Quilting-on-the-Go
Taking It Further

by Carolyn Forster

Landauer Publishing, LLC

'ONE HAS TO KNOW THE TRADITION
WITHOUT BEING STRANGLED BY IT.'
Doris Schmidt, *Suddentsche Zeitung*

Dedication
For Craig and Paul, with love

Projects Copyright© 2013
by Carolyn Forster

This book was designed, produced, and published
by Landauer Publishing, LLC
3100 100th Street, Urbandale, IA 50322
800-557-2144; 515-287-2144; landauerpub.com

President/Publisher: Jeramy Lanigan Landauer
Vice President of Sales and Administration: Kitty Jacobson
Editor: Jeri Simon
Art Director: Laurel Albright
Photographer: Sue Voegtlin

This book is printed on acid-free paper.
Library of Congress Control Number: 2013950341
ISBN 13: 978-1-935726-50-0

Landauer Books are distributed to the Trade by
Fox Chapel Publishing
1970 Broad Street
East Petersburg, PA 17520
www.foxchapelpublishing.com
1-800-457-9112

For consumer orders:
Landauer Publishing, LLC
3100 100th Street
Urbandale, Iowa 50322
www.landauerpub.com
1-800-557-2144

Printed in Singapore: 10 9 8 7 6 5 4 3 2

Contents

Contents

When I began teaching students a portable and more manageable way to quilt their quilts, I had no idea the path it would lead me down. After self-publishing *Quilting-on-the-Go*, I joined with Landauer Publishing who published my second book, *Utility Quilting*.

There are many options for making quilts in smaller sections, either by hand or machine that makes the quilting easier and more manageable. The method I teach is the one I find most comfortable that gives me the best results for the hand quilting I love to do.

I am continually thinking of additional designs that could be made using the quilting-on-the-go technique. In all honesty, part of the reason for *Quilting-on-the-Go, Taking It Further* is because I personally wanted more designs that I could quilt in small sections while I was out and about. The other reason for the book is due to the people I meet who loved the first book and wanted more designs using the quilting-on-the-go technique.

The basic quilting-on-the-go technique, while explained clearly in the first book, got people thinking and asking questions about sashing, block size, and borders.

The questions most frequently asked included:

- How small can I make the blocks?
- Can I sew the blocks together before quilting so there is less joining but still manageability?
- How big can I make the blocks?
- Can I add borders using the same quilting-on-the-go technique?

In *Quilting-on-the-Go, Taking It Further*, I show you how to add borders to your quilts, work with larger and smaller blocks, and which blocks don't require borders. You will also learn to adapt almost any quilt to one that can be quilted-on-the-go, as well as additional ideas for block sashing.

I have included lots of ideas to make your quilting experience more manageable and portable— something to do anywhere!

My students continue to adapt the quilting-on-the-go technique to match their individuality and lifestyle. Several use this type of quilt to take their first steps into the world of machine quilting. That's great! I think when you find a method that boosts your confidence and gives you the results you want, it is a method you should use.

Some of my other students have sewn the blocks into rows instead of quilting each one individually. They then added batting and backing fabric, and quilted the rows just like one big border.

Others have sewn the blocks together into larger units. For example, instead of 16 individual blocks they have sewn four units of four blocks. This gives them only four big blocks to sew together.

It is important to take the pieces of the quilting-on-the-go technique that work for you and implement them in your quilting. Any way is the correct way if it works for you.

Carolyn

Garden Maze and Mayflower Quilt

INTRODUCTION

I LOVE PATCHWORK.

I love that you can always have a block with you to hand-piece whether you're in the garden, at a guild meeting, or on vacation. But for years my quilts were always sitting at home – waiting for me to be there, in that one place at that one time, to quilt them. So while my quilt sat waiting to be quilted, I'd be out and about with my little bag of patches, sewing away, piecing another quilt top to add to the backlog of quilting that already awaited me at home.

Fortunately, the quilting-on-the-go technique solves this problem. Now your quilting can be just as portable as your piecing.

WHAT IS QUILTING-ON-THE-GO?

Quilting-on-the-go is a method of constructing a quilt from lots of small, manageable sections that have been pieced and quilted before the quilt top is assembled. This technique is also referred to as 'quilt-as-you-go' or 'lap quilting.'

By piecing a block on one outing and quilting it the next, you can sew quilts that have been created in small portable pieces. It also means that tacking/basting is a small and manageable task. When it's time to put all those blocks together the quilt is virtually finished. Quilts that you start will now become quilts that you finish before you start the next one.

TIME AND SIZE MANAGEMENT

Quilting-on-the-go is all about time and size management. If you don't have the time or space at home to baste and quilt a full-size quilt, then quilting-on-the-go is the method for you.

THE FOLLOWING ARE ALL REASONS TO TRY QUILTING-ON-THE-GO:

- A lack of space or physical ability to lay a full-size quilt out on the floor to baste the layers together. Quilting-on-the-go eliminates this stage of quiltmaking. You can still sew a full-size bed quilt, but you won't have to lay the entire quilt out to pin-baste or tack it.

- When you first learn to quilt it is generally on small projects. They are easy to handle and quilting is fun. But when you graduate to a full-size bed quilt, it is

a

b

harder to handle the entire quilt at one time and suddenly quilting isn't as much fun. Quilting-on-the-go allows you to quilt each block individually (**a**) and then sew them together to create a larger quilt (**b**) without the aggravation.

- Sometimes when you look at a quilt top, the idea of quilting seems daunting. It looks as though it will take forever. But if you are simply piecing and quilting lots of smaller blocks, a finished quilt seems more attainable.

- You love machine-piecing patchwork and have more ideas than you have time to sew. The machine piecing is fast, but the hand quilting you also love takes longer. You can't fit both into the time you have for yourself in the day. With the quilting-on-the-go technique, you can take the machine-pieced blocks with you and hand quilt during those little pockets of time you have while waiting for appointments or children.

- You want to use piecing and quilting-on-the-go, but don't want to be working on multiple projects. With quilting-on-the-go, you can switch between the two but still be working on one quilt.

- You want to try machine quilting, but don't want to commit to the size and bulk of a big project. Make it a quilting-on-the-go quilt. You can sew a block and quilt it all in the same morning and be well on your way to a full-size quilt by the end of a week.

- Even experienced quilters need portable quilting and the satisfaction of knowing that those individual blocks will end up on as a quilt.

TAKING IT WITH YOU

With the quilting-on-the-go technique, you can take your quilting anywhere you would take hand-piecing. And, of course, you don't have to be out of the house; you can sit and quilt blocks while you're watching television or listening to music. This is certainly more sociable than shutting yourself away with a big quilt in a separate room.

Following are a few 'traveling' suggestions for your quilting-on-the-go projects:

- Car trips (as long as you are the passenger)
- Plane, bus or train journeys
- On vacation, a little relaxing hand quilting won't hurt
- Waiting rooms - doctor, dentist appointments
- Hospital visiting - it's nice to stay a while to keep people company, so why not take the quilting with you?
- Any meeting involving a lot of listening but not much doing
- Waiting to pick up children from after-school activities
- Lunch breaks at work

MAKING EACH QUILT LOOK DIFFERENT

Even though the basic method of construction is the same for quilting-on-the-go quilts, the quilts can all have a different look. My first quilting-on-the-go project had the standard sashing strips around each block. The designs I've developed since are very different. Although the quilts are still put together by stitching a sashing, or frame, around each block, the sashing has become part of the integral design of each quilt. The lines between individual framed blocks become blurred and are sometimes almost completely disguised.

In *Quilting-on-the-Go, Taking It Further* I've tried to include as much variation as possible so you can see the technique's versatility. Of course, you can vary the designs even further by combining different blocks, sashings, and fabric choices.

Some of the sashings in the designs merge into the blocks, due to a careful combination of block and sashing design. Other sashings form secondary designs. When you use the traditional sashing style that isolates the blocks, you can put any block in the center of the sashing. Some block and sashing designs can be combined to create an overall design, for example my Irish Chain variation.

Once you learn the basics of sashing (frames) and fabric selection, all your quilts can be made 'on the go' and they definitely won't look the same. You'll soon be looking at quilts in books and magazines and realize that many can easily be made using the quilting-on-the-go technique.

I've included a bit of history showing that the quilting-on-the-go technique has been around since the late 1800's, so you do not need to feel bad about not quilting the traditional way. You actually are! Also, there are eleven new designs in this book for you to make using the quilting-on-the-go method.

Starry Table Topper

QUILTING-ON-THE-GO: A BIT OF HISTORY

Over the years I have worked on many versions of quilting-on-the-go techniques. I have read books and magazine articles, and seen examples of the techniques in vintage quilts and museums. That is correct—making quilts in small portable and manageable sections is not a new idea.

Quilters have been using small pre-quilted pieces to put quilts together since the 1850's.

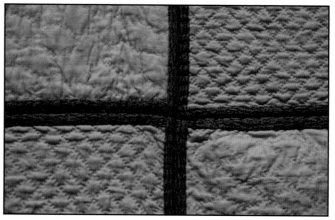

The first quilt I saw put together in the quilting-on the-go style was at the Museum of American Folk Art in New York. It took my breath away. I was certain I was seeing things.

What I found most interesting is there was no mention of the construction technique used in the quilt. However, after looking at it I could see that the blocks and border had each been sewn, quilted, and bound separately and then the parts were sewn together. It is believed that the quilt was made in 1856.

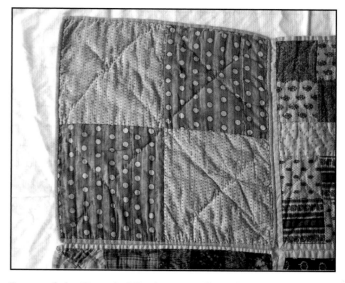

Research by Pamela Weeks, as well as the exhibit of Civil War quilts entitled One Foot Square, Quilted and Bound at the New England Quilt Museum which she curated, clearly illustrates that women have been creating large quilts from small quilted blocks since 1860. The small blocks are bound and stitched together with a whipstitch. There were approximately 70 quilts, often referred to as potholder quilts, discovered in this research project.

Other examples of quilting-on-the-go

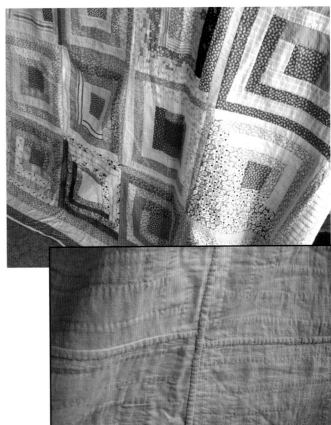

Another quilting-on-the-go technique includes quilts from the 1930's that were sewn as individual pockets containing batting. The pockets were then quilted and put together. I made the quilt shown using this technique. More information on the quilt and technique can be found in the July/August 1998 issue of the Quilter's Newsletter magazine.

The quilt shown is from a Japanese quilter who sewed and quilted the units before joining them together with a ladder-type stitch. No unwieldy quilt to work on, no basting table needed, and no space required to lay the pieces out.

This patchwork quilt from the 1940's has been sewn together in sections. It doesn't have any batting and the blocks were hand sewn and put together with flat-felled seams. The border was then added and machine sewn.

History tells us that quilters have been looking for manageable and portable ways to quilt long before us. Those who dismiss quilting-on-the-go as a non-traditional way to put a quilt together may need to re-adjust their definition of tradition. Similar challenges have always been present in quilt making and similar solutions continue to provide the answers.

Equipment and Supplies

No special equipment is needed for the quilting-on-the-go technique. You will be piecing the blocks and adding the sashing using your favorite hand or machine method. Obviously, if you sew by hand your work is already portable.

BASIC SEWING EQUIPMENT

To make the quilts in this book you will need the same basic sewing supplies all patchwork requires. I don't like endless lists of equipment, as it always makes me wonder, 'did they really need all of that to make those quilts?' So rest assured, the equipment listed is what I use, and probably things you already have.

- Betweens/quilting needles, size 10 or 11, for quilting and hand piecing. Roxanne and John James are favorites.

- Sharps needles, size 5 or 6, for sewing the batting together.

- 100% cotton sewing thread, since you sewing cotton fabric.

- 100% cotton quilting thread, since you are quilting a cotton quilt.

- Glass-headed pins are easy to see and use because of the large heads.

- Large scissors (roughly 8" or 21cm) for cutting fabric.

- Small sharp-pointed embroidery scissors for snipping thread.

- An old pair of scissors for cutting batting. This can dull the blades, so I like to use an older pair and not the ones I use for fabric.

- A3 sheets of template plastic for making templates.

- Marking pencils for marking the fabric when hand piecing and marking quilting designs. I like the Ultimate Marking Pencil™ and the Aquarelle range of water-soluble pencils found in art shops. Remember to keep them sharp.

- Thimbles for hand piecing and quilting. If you find thimbles difficult to use, it's worth persevering to avoid sore fingers. If a thimble doesn't work for you, try to find an alternative finger protection that is comfortable for you.

- Sewing machine with a 1/4" foot for easy, accurate piecing. You will also need a walking, or even-feed, foot for binding the quilt.

- Rotary cutter and mat for fast and accurate fabric cutting.

- Acrylic rulers to use with rotary cutters. The 6" x 24" and 6" x 18" rulers are good sizes to have on hand.

- Jinny Beyer Perfect Piecer for hand piecing, Add-A-Quarter™, or the Omnigrid® 1/2"-wide rulers.

- Heat Press Batting Together™ tape to join the edges of the batting. Just cut the tape to the length you need and gently press it onto the batting with a cool iron. The tape is quick and effective and has no resistance when you quilt through it.

- Bag to hold the quilting-on-the-go work so it's always ready.

- 100% pure cotton patchwork-weight fabric; this kind of fabric works best for piecing, and will help you to achieve the results you see in the book.

- Tacking thread for basting the blocks. If you prefer, you can use safety pins, fusible batting or a spray baste. If you secure your quilt layers with safety pins, try the ones with plastic backs. The backs make them easier to hold. A Kwik Klip™ or serrated grapefruit spoon are also useful tools for protecting against sore fingers.

- Hera™ marker or Chaco liner for marking the quilting lines.

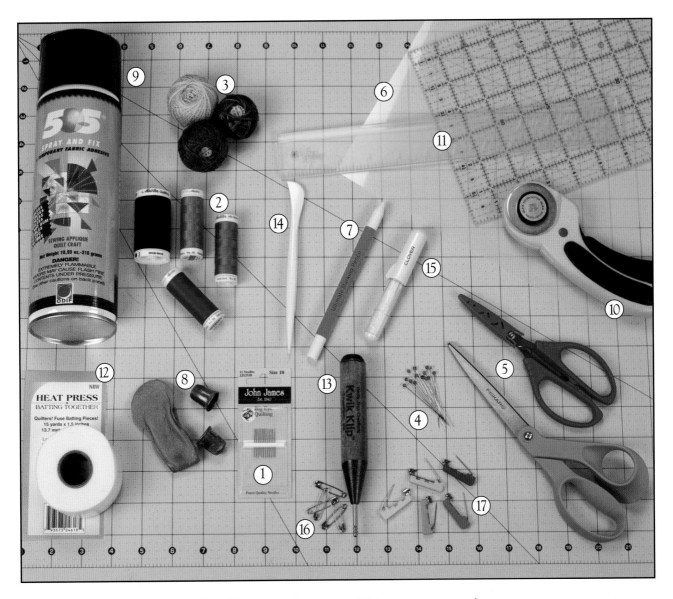

1. Betweens/quilting needles; Sharps needles
2. 100% cotton sewing thread
3. 100% cotton quilting thread
4. Glass-headed pins
5. Large and small scissors
6. A3 sheets of template plastic
7. Marking pencils
8. Thimbles
9. Spray adhesive
10. Rotary cutter and mat
11. Add-A-Quarter™,
    or the Omnigrid® 1/2"-wide rulers
12. Heat Press Batting Together™ tape
13. A Kwik Klip™
14. Hera™ marker
15. Chaco liner
16. Safety pins
17. Plastic backs for safety pins

THE FABRIC

PRE-WASHING YOUR FABRICS

I do pre-wash my fabric. I add it to similarly colored items in my regular laundry. I then dry it on line outside or lightly tumble-dry it until just damp before folding it and putting it in the airing cupboard. Once the fabrics are dry, I store them in clear boxes according to their color families. Since I am going to iron the fabric before I cut it, I don't iron it before I store it.

This is not to say that I have never used a fabric just because it wasn't pre-washed. If I'm at a class and see a fabric that I want in my quilt immediately, I'll purchase it and use it right away.

Colorfastness and shrinkage are the two main concerns people have when it comes to fabrics that haven't been pre-washed.

If I'm ever worried about color running, I put a color-catcher in with the quilt when I wash it. This takes any extra dye out of the quilt during the wash. A word of warning, some pale fabrics have a propensity of attracting surplus dye, whether or not a color-catcher is used. This is generally the fault of the pale fabric, not the dyed fabric. It is an effect that can't be foreseen and unfortunately can't always be reversed.

Fabric shrinkage is not something I worry about. The patches of fabric in my quilts are not huge and since they are well quilted, one piece shrinking a fraction more or less than another has never made any difference to the overall look of the quilt. The quilting itself does act as a stabilizing influence, which is another important reason for a good all-over density of quilting. I select batting that shrinks a bit anyway because I like the slightly puckered effect—it always makes the quilting look good, too. My quilts are made to be used on beds, left on floors, for children to build tents with them and to be snuggled under during the scary bits on TV, so if they're not perfect no one has noticed.

However, if you are making a wallhanging or an exhibition piece where flatness and squareness are important, then you have answered the pre-wash question yourself. You will want to pre-wash everything, even the batting.

CUTTING THE FABRIC

The fabric quantities in the projects are based on the standard 40"-wide cotton fabrics. I have also based the calculations on rotary-cutting the shapes. If you are cutting the pieces out individually with templates, you may want to allow for more fabric.

Rotary-cutting

When you are rotary-cutting fabric, always start with pressed, crease-free fabric. Remember to rotary cut away from you in smooth, firm movements. Don't be tempted to cut several fabric layers at one time. It is better to cut two layers accurately than four layers badly and cutting two layers of fabric is still twice as fast as cutting one layer, or even one piece, at a time.

To cut the shapes required for most pieced patchwork follow the basic instructions shown.

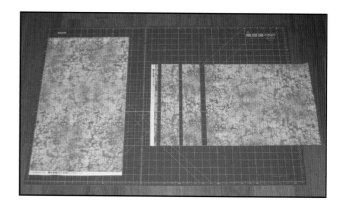

Cutting long sashing strips

Cut a strip of fabric, selvage to selvage, the length of your sashing strip (the example shown is 12-1/2"). Sub-cut the 12-1/2" strip to the width of the sashing strips (the example shown is 2-1/2"). This ensures that the long side of each sashing strip is cut on the most stable, or least stretchy, part of the fabric, which is parallel to the selvage.

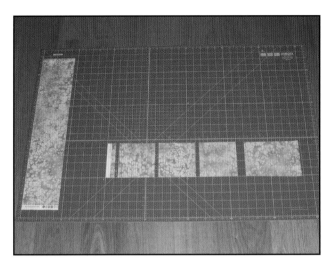

Cutting squares

Cut a strip of fabric, selvage to selvage, the desired width of the squares (the example shown is 4-1/2"). Sub-cut the strip into 4-1/2" squares.

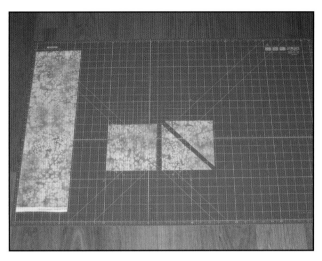

Cutting half-square triangles

Half-square triangles have short sides that are parallel to the straight grain of your fabric. Cut squares, referring to cutting squares. Sub-cut each square in half diagonally to create two triangles.

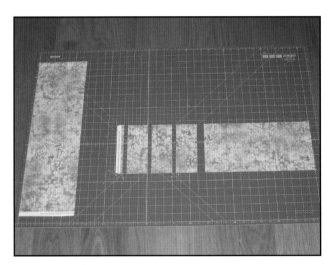

Cutting rectangles

Cut a strip of fabric, selvage to selvage, the desired length of the long edge of the rectangle (the example shown is 6-1/2"). Sub-cut the strip the desired width of the short edge of the rectangle (the example shown is 2-1/2").

Cutting quarter-square triangles

Quarter-square triangles have long sides that are parallel to the straight grain of your fabric. Cut squares, referring to cutting squares. Sub-cut each square in half diagonally twice to create four triangles.

When using the quilting-on-the-go technique you don't have to piece all your blocks before you begin quilting them. If you prefer, you can make one block and quilt it before making the next one. Your finished quilt is essentially one large quilt built up from lots of smaller ones.

You will need to choose the fabric for the back of the quilt at the beginning of the quilt-making process. Because each of the framed blocks has its own backing square, the reverse of your finished quilt will have a number of seams, which will affect your choice of backing fabric. There are various ways to approach the backing fabric selection.

Examples of good choices for backing fabric

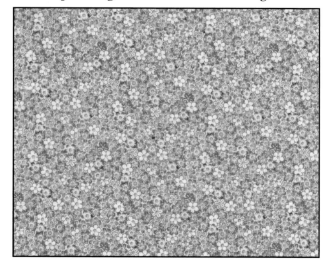

CHOOSING THE FABRIC

The best backing fabric choice is one that hides the seams when the blocks are sewn together. The ideal backing fabric is a small, overall print with no particular direction. These types of prints blur the lines of the seams so you don't really notice them.

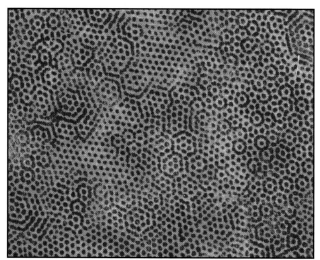

Small, overall print

There are many great fabrics that will work well on the back of your quilting-on-the-go project. When buying backing fabric, allow one fat quarter per sashed block.

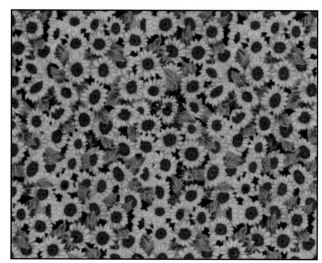

Examples of good choices for backing fabric

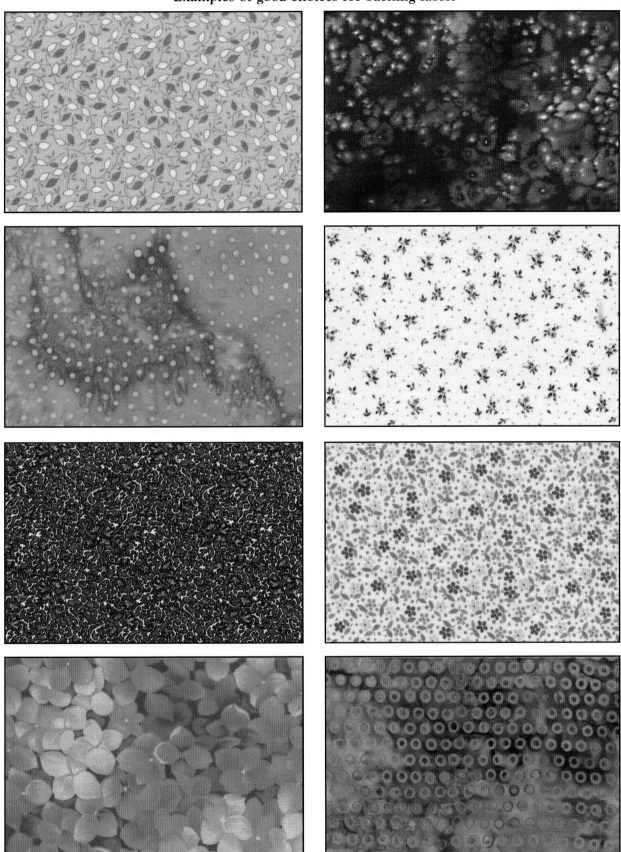

Stripes, checks and toiles aren't necessarily the wrong choices for the back of your quilt, but they require some extra thought and planning.

Large-scale prints are difficult to match, which will give the back of the quilt a fragmented look.

Large-scale print

Full-scale toiles create the same problem as other large prints. Even small-scale toiles tend to be directional, so you need to plan carefully in order to ensure your seams are going in the right direction.

Large, uneven checked prints can be a challenge to match. It is also not easy to camouflage the seams when using a plain fabric on the back.

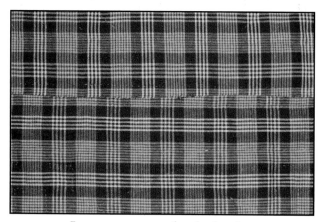

Large, uneven checked print

If you are planning to use a striped fabric, think about the direction of the stripes. Do you want them all going in the same direction or are you happy with the random look your quilt back will have if you leave it to chance?

If you are not worried about hiding seams, but are just grateful to be sewing a quilt that has a chance of getting finished, then try the following method. It is a good way to use those leftover fabric scraps or even the odd 'orphan' fat quarters. This method of using up fabric doesn't hide the seams, so either decide not to worry about the odd ones that don't line up, or leave this type of backing until you've had a bit of practice with quilting-on-the-go.

MAKING A FEATURE OF THE BACK OF YOUR QUILT

This happened to me completely by accident, when I ran out of backing fabric for the blocks on a Turkey Tracks quilt. But, as they say, 'accidents are the father of invention'; I quickly realized I could have some real fun with the back of the quilt by making a feature of the seams rather than hiding them.

Additional backing ideas

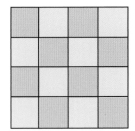

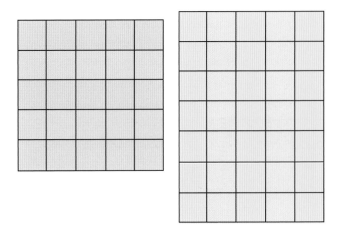

Use two contrasting fabrics for the backing to create a checkerboard effect.

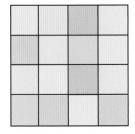

Use all your 'orphan' fat quarters. There always seems to be one that doesn't end up in the front of the quilt. Now you can use them up on the back.

Think how virtuous you'll feel, and how much room there will be in your stash for more fabric.

If you make a nine-block, sixteen-block or twenty-five-block quilt. Design a medallion-style back.

Make the back of the quilt into a strip quilt by using two different fabrics.

Remember, some of these backing ideas will require planning, so you may want to start by concentrating on the quilt front. Also, the design on the back requires you to be 100 percent accurate when lining up your seams—or at least 99 percent. When starting your first quilting-on-the-go project, it may be best to choose one fabric and make sure it is a pattern that hides the seams.

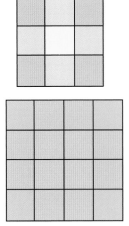

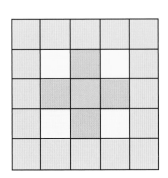

A layer of batting will go between the fabric layers of each block of your quilting-on-the-go project. Choose the batting with care. Making the right choice will allow you to stitch the quilt more easily.

Polyester batting tends to have a more visible loft and the fibers are springier. This springiness can cause problems when you're sewing the quilted blocks together, as the layers tend to shift when you're working with them. For quilting-on-the-go I prefer to use cotton batting. Cotton batting is easy to handle and doesn't have as much loft as the polyester. The patchwork blocks cling to the batting, which makes the layers more stable. Cotton batting is easy to join together when the blocks are quilted and ready to be sewn together into a quilt. Choose cotton batting that is not too stretchy, but is stable and firm.

I prefer to use Hobbs Heirloom® 80/20 cotton blend batting, which is 80 percent cotton and 20 percent polyester. It has all the advantages of cotton batting, but with the added stability of a small amount of polyester. Choose from natural, bleached, or black batting, whichever you feel will work best for your quilt. Another good choice is Hobbs Heirloom® Natural with Scrim. It is good stable cotton batting that is easy to quilt. Scrim is a fine thin layer of stabilizer that is needle-punched into the cotton to help hold the fibers together. It allows you to quilt less densely compared to the same type of batting without the scrim.

Wool batting is heavier than cotton and has a very nice drape. It is easy to quilt, has good insulating properties, and is not too stretchy. Hobbs and Matilda's Own both have good wool and wool-combination batting.

I often have spare pieces of batting left over from larger quilt projects. These leftovers are perfect in my quilting-on-the-go blocks and quilts. When necessary I join batting pieces by machine to make the squares large enough. This is an economical way of working which ensures nothing goes to waste.

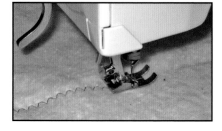

To join pieces of batting, butt the straight edges up next to each other— don't overlap them as this will create a ridge and you want the join to be flat and smooth. Using a neutral thread in the spool and bobbin set the sewing machine to a wide zigzag stitch. Stitch over the butted-up edges with the zigzag stitch, making sure the stitch catches both edges of the batting and holds them firmly together. Square up the piece of newly joined batting to match the size of your backing fabric.

Note: For speed and convenience I use Heat Press Batting Together™ tape to join the edges of the batting. The tape is quick and effective and has no resistance when you quilt through it.

The fabric frames, or sashings, around each block let you know where to stop quilting before the blocks are joined together. After the framed blocks are sewn together, the frames become the sashing and borders of the quilt and can then be quilted at the appropriate time.

When I began sewing quilting-on-the-go quilts I made them in the traditional fashion with plain sashing around the blocks. Gradually I began to play around to see how the sashing, or frames, could influence or change the overall look of a quilt.

I soon realized I could link the sashing design to the block design. By repeating the same block with a related sashing, the block-based design of the quilt blurred into an overall pattern. This effect was enhanced by the fabric choice. I could even use this effect with the traditional sashing even if it wasn't related to the block. The careful choice of fabric blurred the boundaries.

Sashing or Frames

FABRIC CHOICES

The fabric you choose for the frames around your blocks will affect the way the design appears. If the frame is made from the same fabric as the background of the block, then the block design will appear to be floating on the quilt.

If the fabric on the outside edge of your blocks is the same or similar to the fabric of the frame, the blocks and frame will appear as one blended unit. The frame will merge the blocks together, not isolate them.

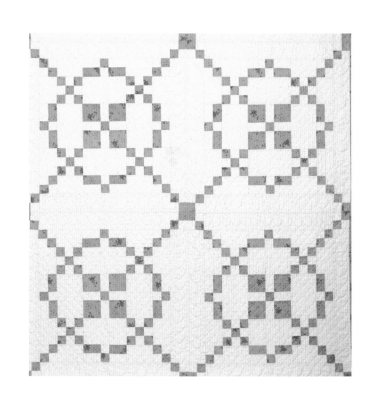

If the frames around the blocks are all different and contrasting, then each block will be isolated by its individual frame.

If you use the same fabric for all the frames but choose one which contrasts strongly with your blocks, then all the frames blend into a single, bold sashing and quilt border.

If this is the first quilting-on-the-go project you've tried, I suggest you stitch a quilt with a simple frame to familiarize yourself with the construction process.

DESIGNING YOUR OWN QUILT-ON-THE-GO

There are dozens of frame, or sashing, ideas to use around your blocks. You can use any of the frames shown around your favorite blocks to create your own quilting-on-the-go project. To ensure the best results, however, follow these guidelines.

- Begin with a simple frame and build up to frames with more pieces.

- The more complex a frame, the more accurate you need to be when you sew it.

- Simple frames have fewer pattern pieces that need matching up when you put the quilt together.

- The more pieces there are in the frame, the more precise you need to be with your sewing.

The basic frames—Courthouse Steps, Broken Courthouse Steps, Partial Piecing and Double Borders—are very forgiving. They can be squared up before you layer the block with backing and batting. This is useful if your block size doesn't match your pattern instructions. For example, the pattern says the block should measure 12-1/2" square, but it actually measures 11-3/4" square.

When you sew one of the basic frames mentioned to this block, add an extra inch to the width plus two inches to the length of the strips. When you measure the framed block it will be bigger than the required 16-1/2" square and you can trim it down to the right size. Problem solved!

FRAMES TO TRY

I have included more than a dozen frames for you to experiment with when designing quilts with your favorite blocks. Examples of the frames are shown.

Refer to Sewing the Patchwork, Framing the blocks on pages 33-39 to find fabric requirements and frame measurements to be used with 12" finished blocks.

BLOCKS WITH NATURAL FRAMES

Many of the quilts I have made have been from blocks with a frame added. The frame added a margin to the block, and showed me where to stop quilting so the blocks could easily be sewn together. The new area between the blocks became the sashing, which was then quilted. This made things nice and straightforward.

However there are many blocks that do not need added frames. When you break the block down into an even grid, 2" or 3" for example, you will find that the block already has a margin around it.

Using blocks with natural frames allows you to create your quilt with a favorite block, without having to think about selecting an appropriate frame.

Mitered Corner Frames

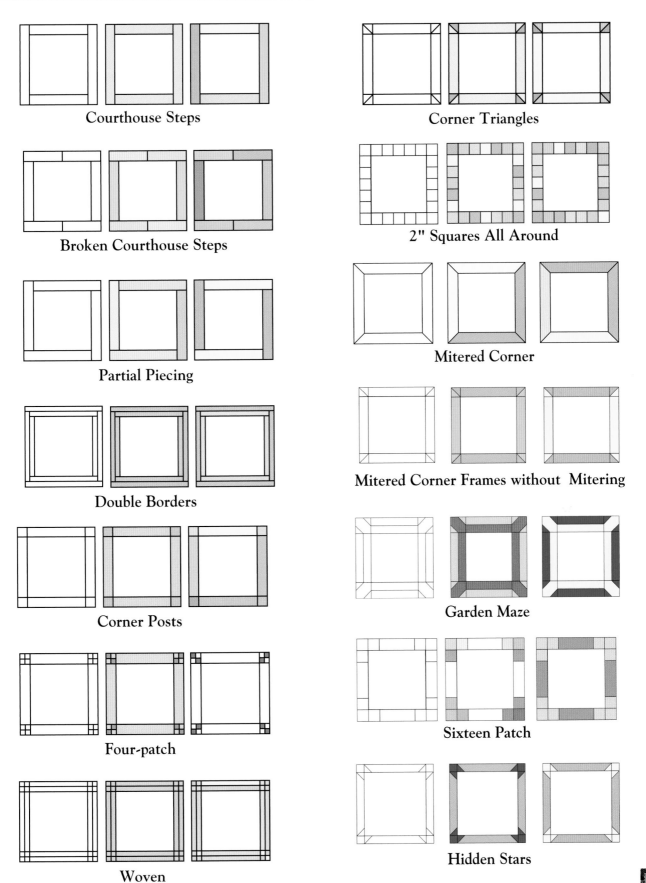

Courthouse Steps

Corner Triangles

Broken Courthouse Steps

2" Squares All Around

Partial Piecing

Mitered Corner

Double Borders

Mitered Corner Frames without Mitering

Corner Posts

Garden Maze

Four-patch

Sixteen Patch

Woven

Hidden Stars

MAKING QUILTS WITH SMALLER BLOCKS

There really is an optimal size to make quilting-on-the-go blocks. If the blocks are too small, the process of putting them together takes more time than the quilting, which doesn't make sense. The solution, if wanting to sew smaller blocks, is to make units of multiple blocks that can be put together with the quilting-on-the-go method.

The Spools Quilt is a good example. The individual blocks are 6" finished, but when put together in three by three units they make great 18" quilting-on-the-go blocks.

As with all quilting-on-the-go blocks, you will need to know where the quilting stops so the top can be put together successfully and then filled in with additional quilting. Since the spool blocks are based on a 2" grid, the outside edge automatically has a 2-1/4" margin around it when the nine blocks are grouped to form the larger block .

Spools Quilt

This is a bit more difficult to see than if we were sewing a quilt like the Garden Maze and Mayflower Quilt. The blocks have a clearly defined frame because they are stitched as separate pieces. This was not done on the Spools quilt where the frame is part of the block design.

Garden Maze and Mayflower Quilt

EXAMPLES OF OTHER BLOCKS THAT CAN BE SEWN TOGETHER IN UNITS:

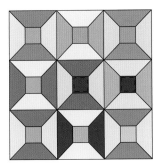

Nine 6" Spools blocks grouped together.

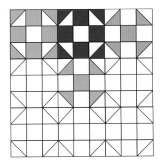

Nine 6" Scrappy Shoo Fly
blocks grouped together.

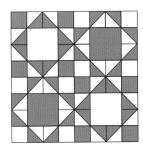

Four 8" Kings Crown
blocks grouped together.

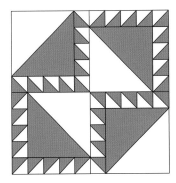

Four 10" Delectable Mountains
blocks grouped together.

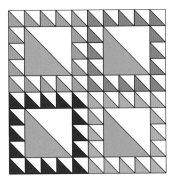

Four 10" Lady of the Lake
blocks grouped together.

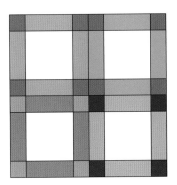

Four 10" Puss-in-the-Corner
blocks grouped together.

DEFINING WHERE TO STOP QUILTING

To define the margin where to stop quilting on the
blocks, experiment with the following suggestions:

- Cut a 2-1/4" x 18" strip from template plastic or
  a piece of cardstock. Align this strip with the
  raw outside edge of the framed block. Mark a
  line on all four sides of the block to define where
  to stop quilting.

- The template strip method will also work well if
  you are designing a whole cloth-style quilt.

- Mark the lines where to stop quilting with a
  contrasting basting thread, thin masking
  tape or chalk.

USING BIGGER BLOCKS

In addition to being asked how small the blocks can be for quilting-on-the-go, I am often asked how big they can be.

If the blocks or groups of blocks get too big the work becomes less manageable and less portable. And really, if it gets too big you are actually just making a quilt the traditional way.

The optimum unit size would be to sew four framed blocks together in squares for a sixteen-block quilt.

You could also sew blocks together in rows before quilting them.

Some quilt blocks just naturally turn out large, such as the blocks in the Burgoyne Surrounded Quilt. I have always admired these quilts, but did not want to cut such small pieces. By basing my quilt design on a 1-1/2" square grid, each unit turned out to be 27" including 3" frames. I only needed nine units to make my quilt, a very achievable number.

USING BLOCKS OF VARYING SIZES

Quilting-on-the-go is great for group quilts. However, there is no way to guarantee that everyone's blocks will be the same size. But, a clever use of the frames can make putting these blocks together in a quilt less of a chore.

When a group of blocks is not all the same size but you want to join them together in a quilting-on-the-go quilt, follow these suggestions:

- Decide what the finished size of all of the blocks needs to be, for example 18".

- Choose a framing fabric. If you use the same fabric to frame all the blocks it will act to unify the quilt. If you choose different fabrics for each block it will give it a scrappier look. Decide which look you want before you start.

- It is likely that different size frames will need to be cut for each block to make their overall size 18-1/2", including seam allowance.

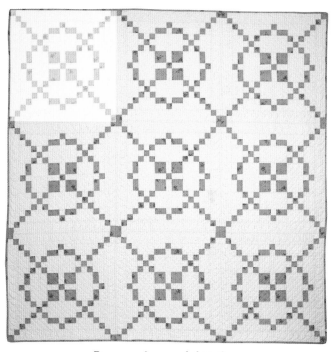

Burgoyne Surrounded Quilt

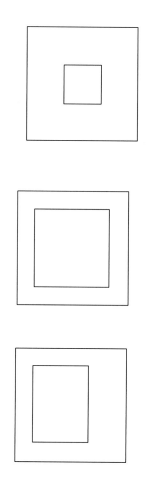

- If you are uncomfortable doing the math, cut generous strips to frame the blocks. Use a square ruler to trim the framed blocks to 18-1/2".

- Since you will likely find that many of the frames will be more than 2-1/4"-wide, you will need to use your ruler gauge.

- Baste the blocks together and mark 2" from the raw edge. This is where you will stop quilting.

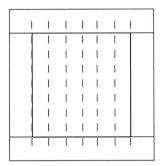

- Choose a quilting design that will unify the quilt blocks. Cross-hatching is a good example. Mark the cross hatching by drawing the first lines through the diagonal of the framed block in each direction. Move the ruler 1" to 1-1/2" from these lines, depending on how dense you want the quilting. Mark the grid all the way to the outside edge of your block. Do this on all of the blocks. When the blocks are put together the lines will all match up.

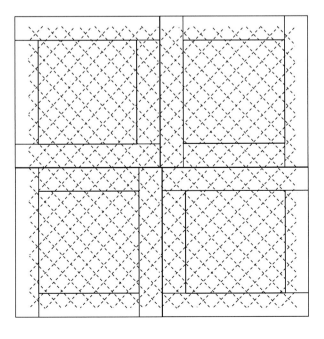

- Another quilting idea would be to mark straight lines starting in the middle of the block and working outward to each side. Make the lines for the quilting go in the same direction as the short frames. Decide how dense you want the quilting and mark accordingly.

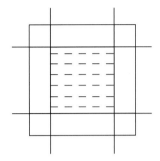

- Join the quilted blocks together alternating the direction of the frames to get a woven effect. Best of all none of the quilting needs to match up.

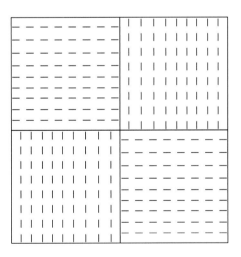

IMPORTANT NOTE: SEAM ALLOWANCES ARE 1/4" UNLESS OTHERWISE NOTED.

SEWING BY HAND

Sewing your quilt by hand has usually meant drawing around templates that excluded the seam allowance, then cutting out the shapes individually and adding the seam allowance as you cut. Jinny Beyer, a well-known American quilter, has been influential in reviving the method of including seam allowances in hand piecing templates. Using this method enables you to rotary cut multiple pieces at one time. Also, since the seam allowance is a uniform width, your hand quilting will always be through a uniform number of layers and will be easier to work. Note: If you judge the seam allowances by eye, and aren't all that accurate, you will find that your seam allowances occasionally stray under the areas you want to quilt and make them too bulky.

If you don't want a solid line, use the Jinny Beyer Perfect Piecer tool to mark an accurate dotted line to follow. This tool has the extra advantage of enabling you to mark the corners accurately so that you don't accidentally sew into the seam allowance.

After some practice you'll find that you won't need to draw the sewing line. You'll be able to judge it by eye.

Now that your cut pieces include the seam allowance you will need to mark the sewing line so your seams are straight. You only need to mark the sewing line on the piece that is facing you as you sew. Use a quilter's quarter ruler or the edge of an acrylic ruler to mark a 1/4" seam line to follow with your stitches.

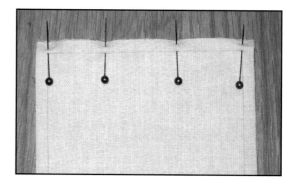

When you're sewing the pieces together, match up the raw edges and pin the pieces together into the seam allowance.

Cut a length of sewing thread roughly the length of your arm or approximately 18". Anything longer is more likely to knot or tangle, and isn't a comfortable length to keep pulling through the fabric. Knot the end of your thread and begin sewing with a backstitch for extra security. Continue along the marked line with a small running stitch, backstitching every 1" or so for extra strength. Finish with two or three small backstitches before cutting the thread, leaving a slight tail.

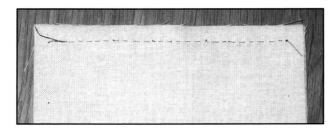

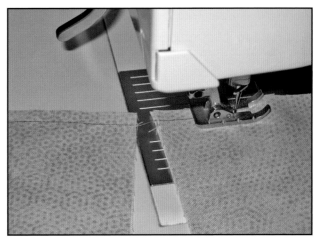

Remember to sew along the marked line or between the dots from point to point, not edge to edge. By not sewing into the seam allowance you will make it easier to position the fabrics where you want them, so you can distribute bulky seams more evenly.

SEWING BY MACHINE

When piecing on the machine, sew roughly 11 stitches to the inch (2.5 on most sewing machines) and exactly 1/4" from the cut edge of the fabric. If you have a patchwork foot this will guide your seam perfectly. If you are using the regular foot on your sewing machine, you may find that you can get an accurate 1/4" seam by shifting the needle position to the right or left so the sewing line is then 1/4" away from the edge of your normal foot. If you use this method of guiding your seam, always remember to set your machine up in the same way before you begin piecing. If you prefer not to move your needle position, mark the throat plate with a piece of masking tape positioned 1/4" to the right of the point where the needle pierces the fabric.

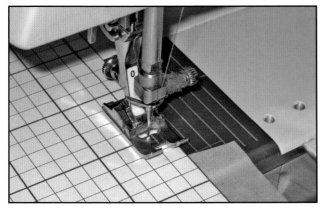

Use a piece of graph paper to measure the distance accurately. Use the tape as your guide when you feed the fabric into the machine.

When you are piecing by machine, start and stop stitching at the edge of the fabric. Use chain piecing when you can, as this saves an enormous amount of thread and time.

Chain piecing involves continually feeding pairs of patches under the presser foot, leaving approximately 1/2" of thread between the pairs. The seamed patches emerge from the machine as a line of bunting or flags, which you can then snip apart.

Get in the habit of using a thread saver. This will, as the name implies, save you thread, but it also means that the machine always has work under the presser foot, making it easier to feed in the next piece of fabric. If you haven't used a thread saver before, use a piece of scrap fabric roughly 2" wide and 3-4" long.

I generally use fabric scraps left over from blocks, or spare lengths of fabric strips I've cut for bindings. Fold the scrap in half and place it under the presser foot. Sew over it before you start seaming the patches and when you finish each seam. This way the thread saver is always under the presser foot when you are not actually stitching, which means that you don't have wasteful ends of thread trailing.

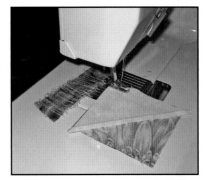

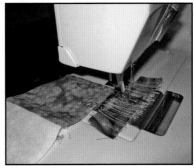

Quick machine piecing techniques

When making the projects in this book I used various quick machine piecing techniques. Some of the quilts use half-square and quarter-square triangles. If you are cutting out the shapes with a rotary cutter, you can often sew the squares together and then cut the squares into half-square triangles. This means the machine sewing is done on a less stretchy piece of fabric and the sewing will be more accurate.

Sewing half-square triangles

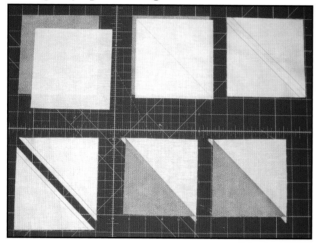

Cut contrasting fabric squares to the size specified in the project cutting instructions, for example 4-7/8" square. Layer two contrasting squares, right sides together, and draw a diagonal line from corner to corner on the wrong side of the lightest color fabric. Sew a scant 1/4" on either side of the drawn line. Cut the square in half on the drawn line. Open the half-square triangles and press the seams toward the darkest fabric.

Sewing quarter-square triangles

Cut contrasting fabric squares to the size specified in the project cutting instructions, for example 5-1/4" square. Layer two contrasting squares, right sides together, and draw a diagonal line from corner to corner on the wrong side of the lightest color fabric square. Sew a scant 1/4" on either side of the drawn line. Cut the square in half along the drawn line. Open the half-square triangles and press the seams toward the darker fabric. Draw a diagonal line from corner to corner on the wrong side of one half-square triangle. Place the half-square triangle with the drawn line on the remaining half-square triangle, right sides together and opposite colors touching. Sew a scant 1/4" seam on either side of the drawn line. Cut on the drawn line and press the seams of the quarter-square triangles in one direction.

Pressing the seams

As a general rule, the seams are pressed toward the darker fabric. If I have given specific pressing instructions within a project that doesn't follow this rule, it is to reduce the bulk of the seam allowances.

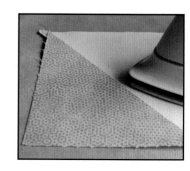

When I press patchwork I always press from the front of the work, moving the iron from the flat piece toward the ridge of the seam allowance. This ensures smooth seams and no little pleats or puckers where the fabric patch buckles up against the seam.

FRAMING THE BLOCKS

Experiment with the following frames when designing quilts with your favorite blocks. Fabric requirements and frame measurements given are to be used with a 12" finished block.

Refer to The Frames on pages 21-25 to review general information before beginning. Arrows indicate pressing direction.

Courthouse Steps Frame

Cut (2) 2-1/2" x 12-1/2" strips and
  (2) 2-1/2" x 16-1/2" strips

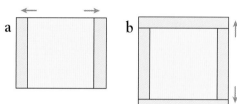

Sew the 2-1/2" x 12-1/2" strips to opposite sides of the 12-1/2" block as shown in step **a**. Press.

Sew the 2-1/2" x 16-1/2" strips to remaining sides of the block as shown in step **b**. Press.

Broken Courthouse Steps Frame

Cut (2) 2-1/2" x 12-1/2" strips and
  (4) 2-1/2" x 8-1/2" strips

Sew (2) 2-1/2" x 8-1/2" strips together to form a unit. Make 2 units as shown in step **a**. Press.

Sew the 2-1/2" x 12-1/2" strips to opposite sides of the 12-1/2" block as shown in step **b**. Press.

Sew the step **a** units to remaining sides of the block as shown in step **c**. Press.

Corner Posts Frame

Cut (4) 2-1/2" x 12-1/2" strips and
  (4) 2-1/2" squares

Sew a 2-1/2" square to opposite ends of a 2-1/2" x 12-1/2" strip to form a unit. Make 2 units as shown in step **a**. Press.

Sew 2-1/2" x 12-1/2" strips to opposite sides of the 12-1/2" block as shown in step **b**. Press.

Sew the step **a** units to remaining sides of the block as shown in step **c**. Press.

Partial Piecing Frame

Cut (4) 2-1/2" x 14-1/2" strips

Sew a 2-1/2" x 14-1/2" strip to one side of the 12-1/2" block. Stop sewing approximately 1" from the edge. The first strip is only partially pieced to the block as shown in step **a**. Press.

Continue sewing the 2-1/2" x 14-1/2" strips to the block as shown in steps **b-d**. Press.

When the fourth strip is attached (step **d**), finish the seam of the first strip as shown in step **e**.

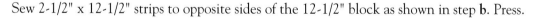

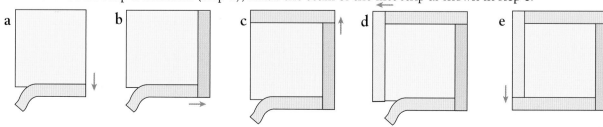

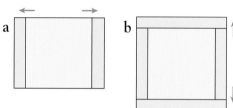

33

Four-Patch Frame

Cut (4) 2-1/2" x 12-1/2" strips and
(16) 1-1/2" squares

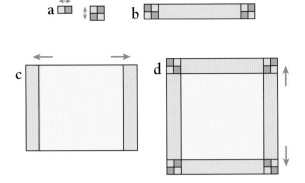

Sew (4) 1-1/2" squares together to form a four-patch as shown in step **a**. Make 4 four-patches. Press seams open.

Sew 2 four-patches to opposite ends of a 2-1/2" x 12-1/2" strip to form a unit. Make 2 A units as shown in step **b**. Press.

Sew 2-1/2" x 12-1/2" strips to opposite sides of the 12-1/2" block as shown in step **c**. Press.

Sew the step **b** units to remaining sides of the block as shown in step **d**. Press.

Woven Frame

Cut (8) 1-1/2" x 12-1/2" strips and
(16) 1-1/2" squares

Sew (2) 1-1/2" x 12-1/2" strips together to form a strip set as shown in step **a**. Make 4 strip sets. Press seams open.

Sew (4) 1-1/2" squares together to form a four-patch as shown in step **b**. Make 4 four-patches. Press seams open.

Sew 2 four-patches to opposite ends of a strip set to form a unit. Make 2 units as shown in step **c**. Press.

Sew step **a** strip sets to opposite sides of the 12-1/2" block as shown in step **d**. Press.

Sew the step **c** units to remaining sides of the block as shown in step **e**. Press.

Corner Triangles Frame

Cut (4) 2-1/2" x 12-1/2" strips and
(4) 2-7/8" squares

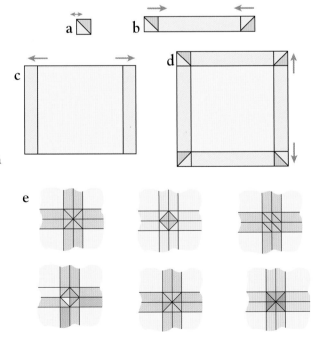

Refer to Sewing half-square triangles on page 32 to make 4 half-square triangles using the 2-7/8" squares as shown in step **a**. Press seams open.

Sew 2 half-square triangles to opposite ends of a 2-1/2" x 12-1/2" strip to form a unit. Make 2 units as shown in step **b**. Press.

Sew 2-1/2" x 12-1/2" strips to opposite sides of the 12-1/2" block as shown in step **c**. Press.

Sew the step **b** units to remaining sides of the block as shown in step **d**. Press.

*Note: With the Corner Triangles frame design, setting the triangles at different angles will produce different effects when your blocks are joined, as shown in step **e**. Choose the design that works best for your project.*

Double Borders Frame

From color 1, cut (2) 1-1/2" x 12-1/2" strips and
(2) 1-1/2" x 14-1/2" strips

From color 2, cut (2) 1-1/2" x 14-1/2" strips and
(2) 1-1/2" x 16-1/2" strips

Sew the 1-1/2" x 12-1/2" color 1 strips to opposite sides
of the 12-1/2" block as shown in step **a**. Press.

Sew the 1-1/2" x 14-1/2" color 1 strips to remaining
sides of the block as shown in step **b**. Press.

Sew the 1-1/2" x 14-1/2" color 2 strips to opposite sides
of the block as shown in step **c**. Press.

Sew the 1-1/2" x 16-1/2" strips to remaining sides of the
block as shown in step **d**. Press.

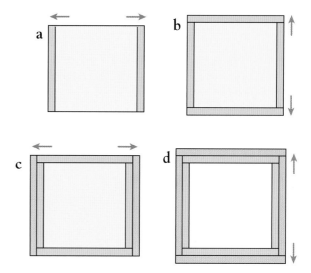

2" Squares All Around Frame

Cut (28) 2-1/2" squares.

Sew (6) 2-1/2" squares together to form a unit. Make 2
units as shown in step **a**. Press seams open.

Sew (8) 2-1/2" squares together to form a unit. Make 2
units as shown in step **b**. Press seams open.

Sew the step **a** units to opposite sides of the 12-1/2" block
as shown in step **c**. Press seams toward
the block.

Sew the step **b** units to remaining sides of the block as
shown in step **d**. Press seams toward the block.

*Note: The Low Volume Irish Chain Quilt on page 74 is a
variation on this method. The 2" square all around frame
can be used with a postage stamp block for a great postage
stamp quilt.*

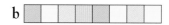

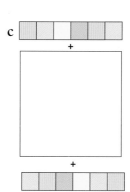

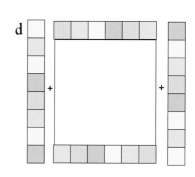

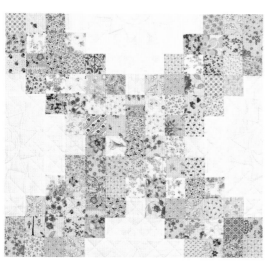

Mitered Corner Frame

From color 1, cut (2) 2-1/2" x 15-1/4" strips

From color 2, cut (2) 2-1/2" x 15-1/4" strips

a

Using the 45-degree line on your ruler, trim the corners off the (4) 2-1/2" x 15-1/4" strips as shown in step **a**.

Fold the 12-1/2" block in half and finger-press the center along each outside edge. Repeat with each of the strips to mark the center as shown in step **b**.

b

Match the center creases on the strips with the center creases on the outside edges of the block. Pin the pieces together at the center point, right sides together, as shown in step **b**.

c

With raw edges aligned and the block on top, begin sewing 1/4" from the edge of the block and stop 1/4" from the opposite edge as shown in step **c**.

Add the remaining strips to the block in the same manner.

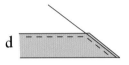
d

> Note: I sew with the block on top because it easier to gauge the 1/4" point. You can mark this point with pencil if it helps you.

After the strips are all sewn to the block it is time to sew the corners. Fold the block diagonally in half and align the raw edges of the frame ends. Begin sewing at the 1/4" point where the frame meets the block. Sew the seam to the outside edge of the frame as shown in step **d**. Repeat on all four corners. Press seams open.

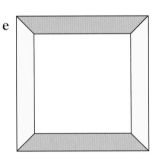
e

Press seams of frames around the block toward the frames.

Sew the same color strips to opposite sides of the block for a Spools Frame. For an Attics Windows frame sew with the same color strips adjacent to one another. See step **e**.

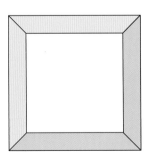

Mitered Corner Frame without mitering

From color 1, cut (2) 2-1/2" x 12-1/2" strips and
(2) 2-7/8" squares

From color 2, cut (2) 2-1/2" x 12-1/2" strips and
(2) 2-7/8" squares

Refer to Sewing half-square triangles on page 32 to
make 4 half-square triangles using the 2-7/8" squares
as shown in step **a**. Press.

Sew 2 half-square triangles to opposite ends of a
2-1/2" x 12-1/2" strip to form a unit. Butt up the
triangles with a matching color strip. Make 2 units
as shown in step **b**. Press.

Sew remaining 2-1/2" x 12-1/2" strips to opposite
sides of the 12-1/2" block as shown in step **c**. Press.

Sew the step **b** units to remaining sides of the block
as shown in step **d**. Press.

*Note: The Mariner's Compass Quilt on page 114
illustrates what a dramatic effect this frame can have
on your quilt.*

a

b

c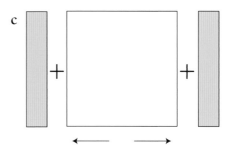

d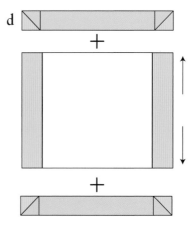

Hidden Stars Frame

Stars will be created when four blocks are joined together. Use the same fabric for the block backgrounds and frames to make the stars in the corners pop.

From block background fabric, cut
(4) 2-1/2" x 12-1/2" strips.

From star fabric, cut (12) 2-1/2" squares.

Draw a diagonal line, corner to corner, on the wrong side of (8) 2-1/2" squares as shown in step **a**.

Place a square on each end of the 2-1/2" x 12-1/2" strips as shown in step **b**. Sew on the drawn line.

Trim off the fabric corners leaving a 1/4" seam allowance as shown in diagram **c**. Press seams open as shown in step **d**.

Sew a 2-1/2" square to each end of two strips as shown in step **e**. Press seams open.

Sew the two shorter frames to opposite sides of the block as shown in step **f**. Press seams open.

Sew the two longer frames to the remaining sides of the block as shown in step **g**. Press seams open.

Note: The stars appear when four framed blocks are sewn together. See step **h**.

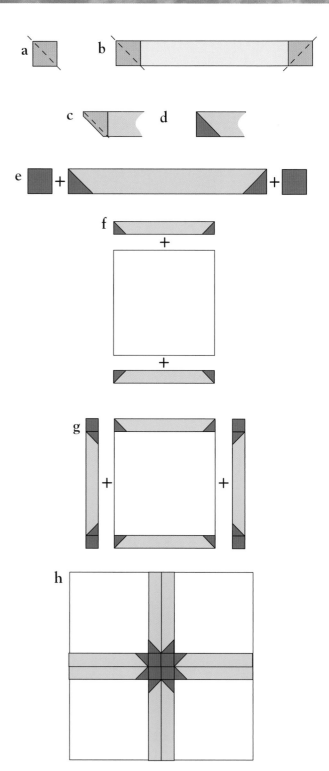

Garden Maze Frame

For best results use the same fabric in the block backgrounds and frames. The lattice fabric should contrast strongly for maximum effect. See the Garden Maze and Mayflower Quilt on page 80 for an example of this frame.

From block background fabric, cut
   (4) 1-1/2" x 12-1/2" strips.
   (8) 1-1/2" squares

From lattice fabric, cut
   (4) 1-1/2" in x 12-1/2" strips
   (4) 2-1/2" squares

Sew a 1-1/2" x 12-1/2" lattice strip and 1-1/2" x 12-1/2" background strip together lengthwise to make a strip set as shown in step **a**. Press the seam towards the lattice fabric. Make 4 strip sets.

Draw a diagonal line, corner to corner, on the wrong side of all the 1-1/2" squares as shown in step **b**.

Lay the marked 1-1/2" squares on the corner of the 2-1/2" lattice squares, right sides together. Sew on the drawn line as shown in step **c**.

Lay a marked 1-1/2" square on the opposite corner, right sides together. Sew on the drawn line. Trim off the excess fabric leaving a 1/4" seam allowance as shown in step **d**. Press seams open to make one unit. Make four units.

Sew a step **d** unit to opposite ends of a strip set as shown in step **e**. Press seams open to make a unit. Make two units.

Sew the remaining strip sets to opposite sides of the block as shown in step **f**. Press seams open.

Sew the step **e** units to the the remaining sides of the block as shown in step **g**. Press seams open.

a

b

c

d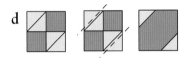

e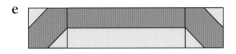

f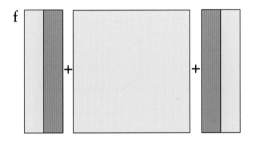

g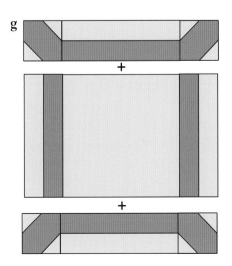

After your blocks are framed, they are ready to be layered, basted, and quilted.

LAYERING AND BASTING THE BLOCKS

Cut the batting and backing fabric for the block 2-1/2" larger than the overall size of the framed block. For example, if

a

the framed block measures 16-1/2" square, then the backing and batting each needs to be cut 19" square (16-1/2" + 2-1/2" = 19"). (**a**)

If you wish, you can use the backing fabric square as a template to cut the batting. (**b**) Remember to unfold the batting 24 hours before you

b

need it to remove any creases and allow time for the batting to fluff up and 'relax.'

Note: Cutting batting can dull the blade of your scissors or rotary cutter. Keep an old pair of scissors, or an old rotary cutter, handy for specifically cutting batting. You will also need them to trim the surplus batting from the blocks when you are stitching them together.

You can layer the batting to cut several squares at once. I don't recommend cutting more than four layers at one time as it makes it difficult to use the scissors.

c

The blocks need to be layered so the batting is sandwiched between the backing fabric and the framed block (**c**). Secure the layers together so they won't move while you are quilting the block. Choose one of the following methods to secure the layers:

- needle and tacking thread
- safety pins (using a Kwik Klip™ or spoon basting for speed)
- tacking gun
- basting spray, such as 505
- iron-on batting

The major advantage to securing individual blocks together is you don't need a large space to spread out and baste the entire quilt.

BASTING WITH NEEDLE AND TACKING THREAD

Lay the backing fabric on a flat surface, wrong side up, smoothing out any wrinkles. Place the batting on the backing fabric aligning the raw edges. Center the framed block on the batting and secure it with pins at the corners and in the middle. Using tacking thread and a Sharps needle size 5 or 6 tack the block as shown in (**d**) and (**e**). Begin your line of tacking with a knot and finish it with a backstitch.

d

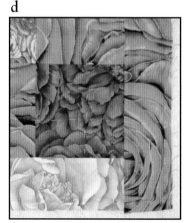

e

The diagram shows the approximate amount of tacking needed on an average size block.

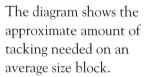

Basting with safety pins

If you are basting with safety pins, you may find it helpful to mark the quilting design on the block before you secure the layers so the pins don't get in the way. Refer to Basting with needle and tacking thread on **f**

page 40 to layer the backing, batting and block. Use safety pins to secure the layers, working from the center outward to ensure the work remains smooth and flat. Pin every 3"-4". (**f**)

To prevent sore fingers use a serrated grapefruit spoon or a Kwik Klip™ tool (**g**) to ease the pin up through the layers. If you want to see the pins more clearly and have something more substantial to grip, use the Quilters Delight® safety pin grip covers. (**h**) Do not place pins where the quilting will be or you will have to remove the pins before you start quilting. With tacking thread, tack **h**

g

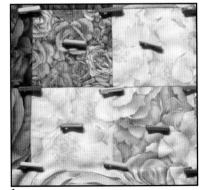

1/4" from the raw edge of the framed block. This final line of tacking helps stabilize the fabric edges when you are ready to join the blocks together. You can also leave the tacking stitches in place after you have removed the safety pins.

Basting with a tacking gun

Refer to Basting with needle and tacking thread on page 40 to layer the backing, batting and block. Pierce the three layers with the needle of the tacking gun coming back up to the front of the work. Click the trigger to release and position the plastic tack. Remove the needle and repeat the process, spacing the tacks evenly across the layers. Do not tack where you know you will have a quilting line. When the quilting is finished, snip through the plastic tags to release them. With tacking thread, tack 1/4" from the raw edge of the framed block.

Basting with basting spray

Lay the batting on a smooth flat surface. Protect the surface with an old sheet or newspaper. Following the manufacturer's directions, lightly spray the batting with 505® or a similar basting

i

spray. Place the backing fabric, wrong side down, on the batting, aligning the raw edges. Smooth the backing fabric from the center outward, repositioning it as necessary. Turn the layers over so the batting is facing up. Very lightly spray the basting spray on the back of the block. Carefully position the block on top of the batting, making sure it is centered. Smooth the block gently to ease out any creases. With tacking thread, tack 1/4" from the raw edge of the framed block. (**i**)

Basting with iron-on batting

Note: This technique only works with fusible batting.

Refer to Basting with needle and tacking thread on page 40 to layer the backing, batting and block. Iron the three layers together. Be careful not to iron the exposed batting, as it will stick to the iron. With tacking thread, tack 1/4" from the raw edge of the framed block.

MARKING THE QUILTING DESIGN ON THE BLOCK

There are many ways to mark a quilt and an endless number of marking tools to help you accomplish the task. Every quilter has a favorite technique or tool when it comes to quilting. Experiment with many types of marking tools to decide which is best for you. If you are at a class or in a quilting group and someone has a marking tool you haven't tried, ask if you can borrow it. This is an excellent way to try out different markers without the expense of buying them all. Ultimately, you will end up with a small selection that you enjoy working with, and which show up on most of your fabrics.

I most frequently use the following tools to mark quilting designs on my framed blocks:

- Ultimate Marking Pencil
- 2H lead pencil
- silver pencil from a quilt shop
- Aquarelle pencils

  Note: These pencils all need to be kept sharp to make sure that they produce a good fine line.

The Chaco chalk marker also does a good job, and comes in various colors. Choose the marker with regard to what will show up clearly on the framed block fabrics. Bear in mind that no marker is guaranteed to come out of the fabric; if you're worried about this, test the marker on a spare piece of fabric first. Remember, the mark doesn't have to be very dark, just bold enough for you to see it while you quilt. Many pencil and chalk marks will disappear during the quilting process, which saves you from having to remove them later. If I am drawing straight lines such as a grid, I use a Hera™ marker with a rotary-cutting ruler as my guide.

Learn to outline quilt by eye. It might sound scary, but once you try it there will be no going back. Begin by using pieces of 1/4"-wide masking tape as a guide to train your eye. As you become more familiar with the 1/4" measurement, use the edge of the seam allowance under the patches as an invisible guide for the needle.

QUILTING THE BLOCKS

There are a number of ways to approach the quilting and construction of your quilt. Two of my favorite methods are listed.

- As you piece each individual block, frame it and then quilt it. When all the blocks are quilted, you can decide on the quilt layout and sew the framed blocks together row by row.

- Decide on the quilt layout before you begin quilting the framed blocks. If you choose this method, you will need to label all the blocks, which can then be quilted in sequence, row by row. Once the first row of blocks has been quilted you can join them together and quilt the sashing. After completing the second row, it can be sewn to the first row and their sashings quilted. Continue quilting the blocks and row sashings in this manner. By the time the last row of individual framed blocks has been quilted, the rest of the quilt is completely quilted and just waiting for the final row.

There is no right or wrong way; simply choose the method that works best for you.

No matter how the quilt will be quilted overall, the quilting design at this stage doesn't extend into the frame by more than 1/4"-1". A good rule of thumb—the newer you are to the quilting-on-the-go technique, the less you want to quilt into the frame. If this is the first time you have used the technique you will find it easier to sew the framed blocks together if you have a minimum amount of quilting in the frame. **(a)** The more quilts you make with this technique, the more quilting you can put in the frame before sewing them together.

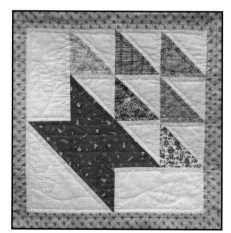

a

Leaving most of the frame clear of quilting allows the blocks to be sewn together easily. Once the blocks are joined into rows, the quilting on what becomes the sashing and borders will be a cinch, as it's all designed to be worked in one direction as the quilt comes together in sections.

Note: Sometimes part of the quilting design in the framed block links up across the blocks. When this happens, I don't tie off the thread I'm using for quilting each block. I leave the thread loose so when I have sewn the frames together, I can continue quilting across the sashing with the same thread. This is a handy technique for those who don't enjoy the tying-off process.

At this stage of the quilt construction you are only quilting the framed block, so use the suggested quilting design within each project or choose your own design to fit into the same space. This is where you start to benefit from your portable quilting; the framed blocks are now ready to be quilted in those 'spare' moments when you are out and about, or quilting-on-the-go. On the other hand, if you have always wanted to try machine quilting your projects, this is the ideal way to start without having to manipulate a large quilt under the machine.

Keeping it portable and ready to go

b

I keep my work ready to go in a bag by the front door. When I'm getting ready to go out, I pick up my coat, my keys, and my quilting. When I get home, I take out my finished work and replace it with a new piece to be worked on during my next outing. Now there's no delay when going out and taking my quilting along.

You will need a few additional quilting supplies in your bag: (**b**) a thread cutter, quilting thread, thimbles, and extra needles (Roxanne™ quilting needles come in a small cylinder which is handy to keep in your bag). You may want to have a few threaded needles ready to use if you find needle threading hard on your eyes.

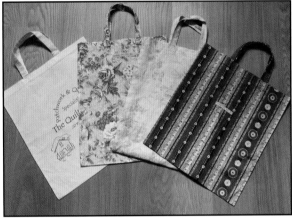
c

I began keeping my work in a bag from my local quilt shop since it was just the right size. However, one day I got to thinking that if they could have their own bags, so could I. In the classes I teach, we have had great fun seeing the bags everyone makes—some of the students make a new bag for each new quilting-on-the-go quilt they make. The quilters' bags are as individual as their quilts (**c**). If you'd like to make your own bag, instructions are provided on page 44.

A bag for carrying your Quilting-on-the-Go

Fabric Requirements

1-1/8 yards (1m) of fabric for bag body and handles
Note: If you are using patterned or directional fabric, purchase extra yardage.

Cutting

- Cut (1) 15" x 36-1/2" rectangle for the bag body.
- Cut (2) 2-1/2" x 15-1/2" rectangles for the handles.

Sewing the bag together

1. Fold the bag fabric in half, wrong sides together. Sew 1/4" seam up each long side of the folded bag fabric.

2. Turn the bag inside out so the right sides of the fabric are facing and the raw seam edges are inside the bag. Sew along the side seams to enclose the raw edges. This French seam automatically neatens the raw edges.

3. At the open end of the bag, turn the fabric to the outside to create a 1-1/4" hem. Press. Turn the raw edge under 1-1/4", pin, and machine sew close to the fold of the hem.

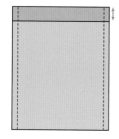

4. Fold 1/4" hem to the wrong side on both long sides of each handle rectangle. Fold each strip in half, wrong sides together, and machine stitch along the edge of each long side.

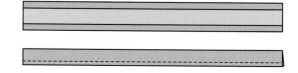

5. Using pins mark 4" from the side seams. Position one end of the handle on the inside upper edge of the bag next to the pin; turn under the raw edge and pin in place. Machine stitch the end of the handle position with a grid of stitched lines, following the stitching sequence shown in the diagram.

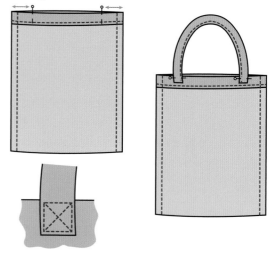

6. Repeat the stitching on the remaining handle ends to secure them to the bag. Turn right side out and press. Label your bag if desired.

QUILT SIZE

'HOW BIG SHALL I MAKE MY QUILT?'

Although each project in this book is a specific size, there is no reason you can't adapt the size to fit your needs. The simplest way to do this is to make more or fewer blocks depending on your requirements. Quilting-on-the-go is a versatile and flexible method of quiltmaking.

To assist you in determining how many framed blocks you need for specific quilt sizes, I've worked out the following formula based on the most popular sizes of bed coverings. The finished framed block size I have used is 16" since that is the finished size of most of the framed blocks in the project section.

Cot—24" x 50"
Sew **six** blocks to make a 32" x 48" quilt.

Throw—48" square
Sew **nine** blocks to make a 48" square quilt.

Cot-bed—47" x 55"
Sew **twelve** blocks to make a 48" x 64" quilt.

Larger throw—64" square
Sew **sixteen** blocks to make a 64" square quilt.

Single bed—55" x 79"
Sew **twenty** blocks to make a 64" x 80" quilt.

Double bed—79" square
Sew **twenty-five** blocks to make an 80" square quilt.

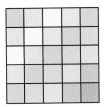

King-size bed—89" x 87"
Sew **thirty-six** blocks to make a 96" square quilt.

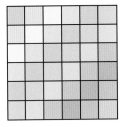

Super-king-size bed—102" x 87"
Sew **forty-two** blocks to make a 96" x 112" quilt.

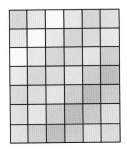

DETERMINING YARDAGE

After you have made some of the projects in the book you will probably want to start creating your own quilting-on-the-go designs. It is always helpful to determine how much fabric you need before starting a project.

Fortunately this is a simple process without any complicated calculations or tables and graphs to consult.

'How much fabric will I need for the blocks?'

To determine how much fabric I need per block, I base my calculation on a fat quarter. If my surface area per block is equivalent to one fat quarter, made up of two fat eighths or smaller pieces, then a fat quarter per block will be enough.

'How much fabric will I need for the frames?'

When buying yardage for the block frames I work on the basis of 6" per block for the frame in one fabric. For example, if I am sewing a 16 block quilt, I will need a total of 96" of fabric (16 x 6 = 96). Or, if working in metric for the same size quilt, allow 15cm per block in one fabric, which is a total of 240cm/2.4m of fabric (16 x 15 = 240).

Or, calculating in fat quarters again, one fat quarter will be enough to frame one block with some fabric left over.

'What size batting will I need?'

For most of the designs in this book you will need to cut 19" squares of batting. For simplicity , when I am determining how much batting I need I usually think in terms of 20" squares. I know the squares will really be a bit smaller, but I'm no good at multiplying in 19's. For example, when I read a queen-size batting packet it says the batting is 90" x 108", so...

- 20" divides into 90" four times
- 20" divides into 108" five times
- 4 x 5 = 20. Therefore I know I will be able to cut (20) 20" squares from a queen-size batting.

Remember, as a bonus you can join the spare pieces of batting together to make more squares for another project. Refer to page 20.

'What about the backing squares?'

For every block in the quilt you will need approximately one fat quarter of backing fabric. A fat quarter measures roughly 20" x 22". You can cut your backing square, which is usually 19" square, from the fat quarter.

'Free' backing squares

If you're cutting the backing squares for your quilt from continuous yardage, as opposed to using fat quarters, you can gain spare squares in a similar way to the spare batting squares.

After you have cut two backing squares from the full width of the fabric, you will have a strip of fabric left over that measures approximately 19" x 7". You will gain a spare strip roughly every half yard. For example, when you cut six backing squares from 1-3/4 yards of fabric, you will have three spare strips. If you sew them together and press the seams open, you will have a backing piece measuring 19" x 20" ready to be squared up for a backing as needed.

- **1-5/8 yards (1.5m)** of fabric yields...
  six whole backing squares
  and **one** joined
  = **seven** in total

- **3-3/8 yards (3m)** of fabric yields...
  twelve whole backing squares
  and **two** joined
  = **fourteen** in total

- **4-7/8 yards (4.5m)** of fabric yields...
  eighteen whole backing squares
  and **three** joined
  = **twenty-one** in total

- **6-1/2 yards (6m)** of fabric yields...
  twenty-four whole backing squares
  and **four** joined
  = **twenty-eight** in total

- **8-1/4 yards (7.5m)** of fabric yields...
  thirty whole backing squares
  and **five** joined
  = **thirty-five** in total

- **9-7/8 yards (9m)** of fabric yields...
  thirty-six whole backing squares
  and six joined
  = **forty-two** in total

PLANNING THE LAYOUT

Before you begin sewing the quilted blocks together, you need to plan the quilt layout. Lay the blocks on the floor, a bed, or any flat surface large enough to accommodate the layout. Arrange the blocks in different combinations until you find a quilt layout you are happy with. (a)

b

c

You can also buy a set of pre-marked labels called Tag-A-Quilt. (b and c) These can be used over and over again to label the blocks by number and row. They pin on easily and save you the time and trouble of drawing out a grid and transferring the information.

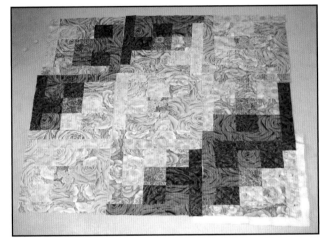

a

If you are having difficulty deciding on the layout, step away and come back to it later. You will find the blocks look quite different after you take a break.

If your quilt layout is still not coming together, you may want to try viewing it in a different way. To obtain a new perspective, use a reducing glass to create distance between you and the quilt. Looking through the viewfinder of a camera will have the same effect. If the quilt is on a bed in a room with a mirror, look at the quilt layout indirectly via the mirror for another angle.

Once you have decided on the layout, you will want a record of your chosen design. Take a photo and print it out for a permanent color and block placement record. Another simple way to record the layout is to draw a rough grid of the quilt on paper and number the squares. Write the number from each square onto a piece of paper and use a safety pin to secure it to the matching framed block.

After you have photographed or labelled your blocks, stack them so they are ready to be sewn together. (d)

d

JOINING THE BLOCKS

Take two adjacent blocks from the beginning of the first row and remove any tacking, safety pins or plastic tacks. Do not remove the lines of tacking on the outside edges of the framed block. Leave these in place until you are ready to join those edges or bind the quilt. They will serve to stabilize the framed block.

Joining the Blocks continued

1. Remove the tacking lines from the edges of the blocks you are sewing together. Fold the batting and backing fabric away from the front of the framed blocks. You may wish to pin it to keep the layers out of the way. (**a**) Layer the front of the blocks, right sides together, and pin.

a

2. Sew the front of the blocks together. (**b**) Remove any pins.

3. Working on the front of the block, press the seams in one direction—press toward the frame with the fewest seams. Use the tip of the iron or a small travel iron to press. (**c**) Avoid pressing the batting and the rest of the quilted block.

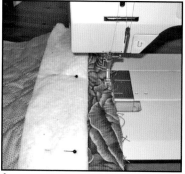

b

I prefer to work with the quilt row over an ironing board during its entire construction.

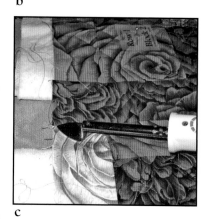

c

The narrowness of the board means that the weight of the work will fall away over the edge of the board, keeping the sashing smooth and flat while still leaving the work easily accessible. An added advantage is the ironing board can be adjusted to a comfortable height to work. The cotton cover also acts to keep the quilt in one place, preventing it from sliding around.

4. Place the joined pair of blocks right side down on a smooth, flat surface. Remove any pins that were holding the batting and backing away from the seam. Smooth down the first piece of batting in the same direction as the seam. This will ensure that you can smooth the batting down without disturbing the direction of the pressed seam. Smooth the other piece of batting over the top of it. The edges of the batting will overlap.

Keeping the batting layers overlapped, cut them together in line with the front seam, using the seam as a guide for the lower blade. (**d**) This will keep you from over-trimming the batting. The two pieces of batting will meet above the front seam, so you won't be pulling the edges to try and make them meet or discover you haven't trimmed off enough and have bulging and overlapping edges. (**e**) Discard the thin cuts of batting.

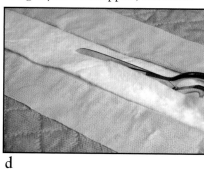

d

e

5. Thread a size 6 Sharps needle with a length of cotton thread in a neutral color to match the batting. Knot the end of the thread. Work with the seam parallel to your body and use a ladder/suture stitch to hold the edges of the batting pieces together. (**f** and **g**)

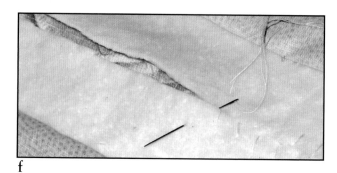

f

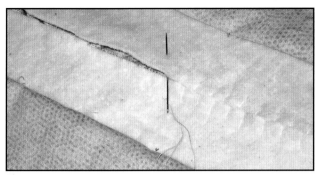

g

Do not allow the batting edges to overlap as this will pull up the front of the quilt and the sashing won't lie flat and smooth.

Work from right to left (if you're right-handed) to draw the two sides of batting together. You do not need to sew the whole length of batting together. Begin where the frame of the block on the front of the quilt starts and finish where the frame finishes. The batting that isn't sewn together will be trimmed away when the rows of blocks are joined together.

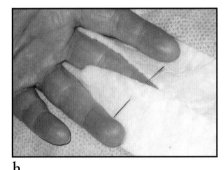

Be careful not to sew through the front of the quilt with your stitches. I sew the batting together with my left middle finger under the join of the two pieces of batting as I work to guide the needle. (h) This also stops me from catching the stitches on the front of the quilt.

h

If you are concerned about catching the front stitches, cut a piece of template plastic 2" x the length of an A3 sheet. Insert

i

this between the batting and the front of the quilt so your stitches can't catch the front of the quilt. They will be deflected by the template plastic. Slide the plastic out when you are finished stitching the batting. (i)

6. When joining the backing fabric together, use the join line in the batting to guide the position of the seam down the backing pieces. The join in the batting aligns with the seam on the front of the quilt, meaning the seam line on the back will also align with the front seam. This will be useful when you join the rows.

7. The excess backing fabric needs to be trimmed so there are no bulky seams or excess seam allowances. This will make things easier when you quilt the sashings. Smooth one piece of backing fabric flat onto the batting. Fold back the edge of the fabric and finger-press the fold along the seam of the batting. You may use pins if it is easier for you. Trim the folded back fabric leaving 1/4" from the fold. (j) This is the 1/4" seam allowance. Repeat with the second piece of backing fabric. (k). Remove the pins when you are finished. Keep the trimmed strips of fabric for strip and string quilts.

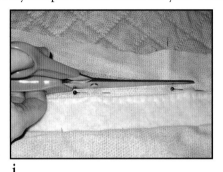

j

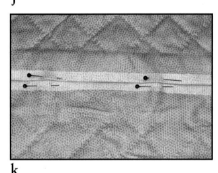

k

8. Smooth one of the backing fabric pieces down onto the batting. (1) The first piece of fabric that you smooth down will dictate the direction of the bulk of the seam allowance. Make sure it is going in the opposite direction of the seam allowance on the front of the quilt.

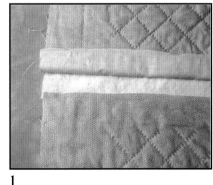

l

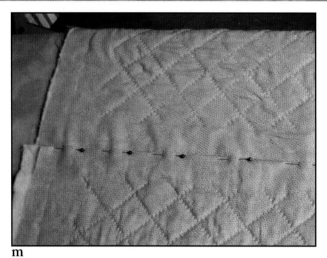

m

9. Smooth the remaining piece of backing fabric down over the first piece. Fold the raw edge under 1/4". The fold should be directly above the seam on the front of the quilt, with the seam allowance going in the opposite direction. Pin the folded edges in place, working from the middle of the block out toward the edges. (m) This will ensure the seam doesn't become twisted or uneven.

10. I use a quilting needle and sewing thread the same color as the backing fabric to sew the seams together. Stitch using a shallow appliqué stitch. (n) Be careful not to catch the batting in the seams for the first

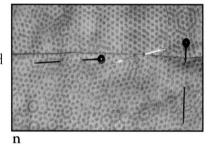

n

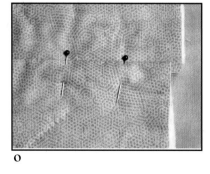

o

and last 2". (o) You need to be able to fold the backing fabric away from the batting when you join the rows of the quilt together. You can insert the piece of template plastic between the backing fabric and the batting to protect the batting from being caught in the stitches.

11. Continue to join the remaining blocks in the row in the same way. Make sure the seams on the back of the quilt row face the opposite direction of those on the front of the quilt.

QUILTING THE SASHING

Quilt the sashing frames between the blocks, stitching to the margins of quilting at the top and bottom of the framed blocks. (a and b)

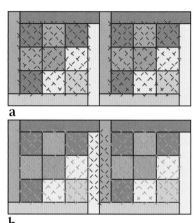

a

b

If you are working on a row of blocks that is the border of the quilt, you can quilt all the way to the outside edge. You can even quilt along the border at this stage (c) or leave it until the entire quilt is complete.

c

This stage of the quilting is also quite portable. A row of blocks can easily be rolled up and put in your bag for quilting-on-the-go.

JOINING AND QUILTING THE ROWS

After the first row of blocks is joined, join and quilt the second block row in the same way. Remember to have the seams on the front and back of the quilt laying opposite those in row one. This helps distribute the bulk of the fabric at the joins and makes for neat seams.

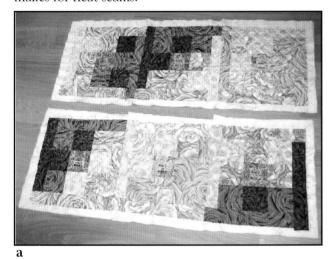

a

Once you have created the first two rows of the quilt, and quilted between the blocks (**a**), you can join them together. This is done in the same way the single blocks were joined (page 47). You are simply working on a longer row.

1. Remove any tacking on the edges that are to be joined. Pin the fronts of the two rows, right sides together, making sure the seams on the front of the quilt match up. Pin where the seams meet. The seams should be facing in opposite directions. (**b**) Sew the rows together, removing the pins as you sew.

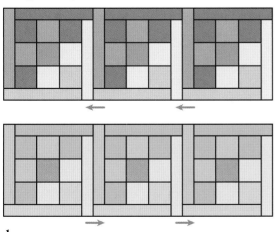

b

2. Press the seam in one direction, ideally toward the first row or top of the quilt. Make sure you press all subsequent long seams in the same direction, toward the top of the quilt. (**c**) This will make the task of assembling all the rows easier.

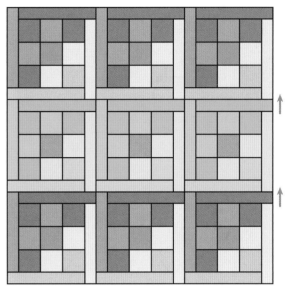

c

You will find that as the quilt grows, the bulk of it will always be draped away from you, so the only bit on your lap, table or ironing board workstation is the row you're working on. You will definitely see the advantage in this as you join multiple rows together.

3. Trim the batting as shown on page 48 and sew the pieces together. (**d**)

d

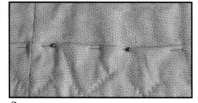

Joining and Quilting the Rows continued

4. Trim the backing fabric as shown on page 49. Pin the fold of the backing fabric, beginning at the seam junctions. (e) These should be facing in opposite directions (f) and nest together to form neat intersections. (g)

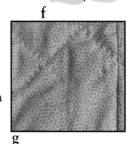

e

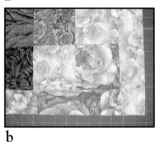

f

The seam junctions on the back of the quilt should match up neatly, because the seams on the front of the quilt do. If they do not match up, don't worry. That is why you chose a backing fabric to camouflage the seams.

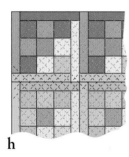

g

To alleviate this problem, check to see how careful you were when you trimmed the batting. Does the batting join line match up with the seam on the front of the quilt? Do the seams on the front of the quilt meet to make perfect junctions? If not, you will know where to take a little more care with your next quilt.

5. Stitch the long seam from start to finish. You won't need to turn under any fabric at the ends of the seams, as these are the borders of the quilt. You can now quilt along the sashing strip you have created between the two rows, stitching from edge to edge (h).

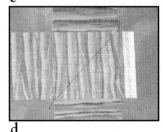

h

Repeat the process of making rows, joining and quilting the rows until the quilt is complete.

QUILTING THE BORDERS

Remember, you can quilt the border area as you create it. If you work methodically, by the time the last row goes on the quilt, the only bits left for you to quilt will be the sashing between the final two rows and the remaining border on the outside edge.

BINDING THE QUILT

Once the quilt is finished it is ready to bind. (a) I like to use a double-fold binding with mitered corners.

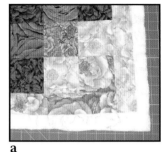

a

I cut the binding strips on the straight of grain, not the bias. I find this helps keep the edges straight and the strips less likely to ripple. If you like you can machine sew a narrow zigzag all the way around the edge of the quilt for extra stability before applying the binding.

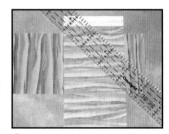

b

Remove any remaining tacking from the edges of the quilt, square up the corners, and trim any extra batting and backing using a rotary cutter and ruler. (b)

Making the binding

1. Cut binding strips 2-1/2" x width of fabric. Lay one strip over another, right sides together, creating a right-angle with approximately 1/2" overlapping. (c) You do not need to trim the selvage yet, as the extra fabric is trimmed off in the process of joining the strips. Draw a diagonal line on the top strip.

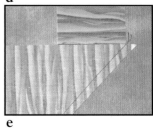

c

d

e

2. Stitch from corner to corner on the diagonal line. (d) You can chain-piece the seams all at once to create the entire length of binding. When all the strips have been stitched, snip the threads between the piece and trim the extra fabric, leaving a 1/4" seam allowance. (e)

3. Press diagonal seams open. (**f**) Fold and press the strip in half lingthwise, wrong sides together. (**g**)

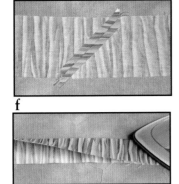

f

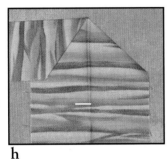

g

Attaching the binding

4. Press the beginning of the binding strip as shown. (**h**) This will create a guideline for the bias join when the beginning and end of the binding come together in step 10.

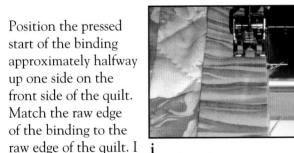

h

5. Position the pressed start of the binding approximately halfway up one side on the front side of the quilt. Match the raw edge of the binding to the raw edge of the quilt. I use a walking or even-feed foot when sewing on the binding. (**i**) Line up the right edge of the foot with the raw edges to determine the width of the finished binding. Begin sewing approximately 2" from the pressed starting point. (**j**)

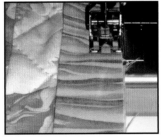

i

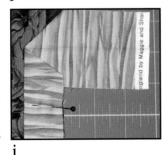

j

6. Continue stitching a straight line toward the corner of the quilt. Stop sewing 1/4" away from the corner of the quilt. (**k**) Backstitch to secure the stitches.

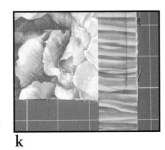

k

7. Take the quilt out from under the presser foot. Fold the binding away from the quilt, aligning it so the raw edge of the binding is in line with the raw edge of the next side to be bound. (**l**) Fold the binding so it lies along the new side to be bound. The fold you have made will sit neatly in the corner you have just negotiated. (**m**)

l

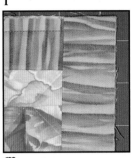

m

8. Start sewing again at the raw edge of the quilt to secure the fold and miter at the corner. (**n**) Continue sewing the binding along the side of the quilt, mitering the corner as before.

9. Continue stitching around the edge of the quilt. Stop sewing approximately 4" from where you began stitching.

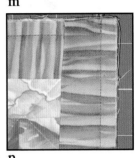

n

Joining the ends

10. Leave the needle in the work to act as an anchor. (**o**) or remove the quilt from under the presser foot if it is easier. Open the beginning binding, strip (see step 4), wrong side of fabric facing up. Trim along the biased fold line, leaving a 1/4" seam allowance. Refold the strip and realign it on the raw edge of the quilt.

o

Binding the Quilt continued

11. Flatten the unsewn end of the binding strip over the folded end. Fold back the unsewn end at a 45-degree angle to match the angle of the fold underneath. (**p**) Trim the extra fabric leaving a 1/4" overlap. Insert the overlap into the beginning of the binding strip. (**q**)

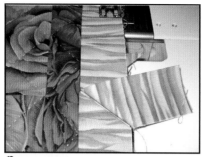

p

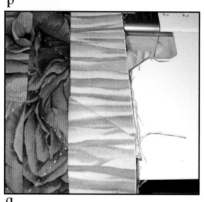

q

12. Begin sewing again at the point you stopped. Continue stitching over the join until you have overlapped the beginning of the stitching line. Secure the threads and remove the work from the machine. (**r**)

r

Hand-finishing the binding

13. Turn the folded edge of the binding over to the back of the quilt covering the raw edges of the quilt. Pin into place. When you come to a corner, the binding should lie in a crisp miter. (**s**) For a nice flat corner, the bulk of the miter should fall in opposite directions on the front and back of the quilt. Using a thread that matches the binding fabric, slipstitch the binding into place. (**t**) Use small stitches to sew up and down each mitre (front and back) and to close the binding where it overlaps. Insert a label into the binding as you secure it if you wish.

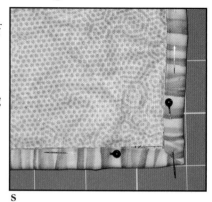

s

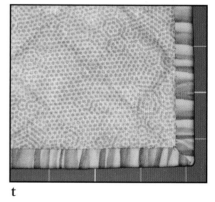

t

I am often asked what to do with the extra batting and fabric pieces that are trimmed from the blocks during the quilt construction process. I suggest cutting the batting into smaller scraps and using it to stuff pincushions and other small projects.

I save the fabric strips to create string blocks for more quilts. String blocks are made with fabric strips of varying lengths and widths. To keep the strips stable as they are sewn together, I stitch them on a leave-in foundation, such as Vilene. This stabilizes the strips and make the blocks easier to stitch. There are many different techniques to make string blocks, but this is my favorite.

MAKING STRING BLOCKS

1. Cut a 6-1/2" square of leave-in foundation.

2. Lay a fabric strip, right side up, diagonally from corner to corner across the center of the foundation square. Use a dab of water-soluble glue to hold the strip in place if desired.

3. Make sure the corners of the foundation are covered by the fabric strip. This will ensure you will not have a seam going through the corner.

4. Layer a fabric strip, right side down, on the center strip with raw edges aligned. Stitch the strips together sewing through the fabric and foundation.

    Tip: If the added strip overlaps the opposite edge of the center strip, finger press it out of the way.

5. In the same manner sew a second strip to the opposite side of the center strip.

Making String Blocks continued

6. Press the strips.

7. Continue adding fabric strips until the foundation square is completely covered.

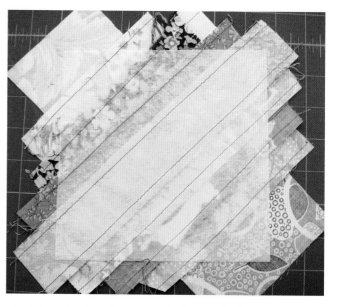

8. Turn the block over and place a 6-1/2" square ruler over the foundation square.

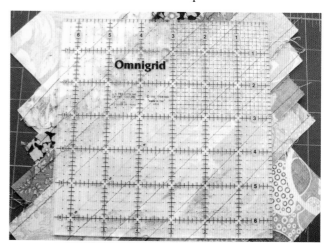

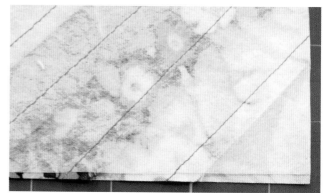

9. Trim the block to 6-1/2".

Note: Do not be concerned if the foundation is now a bit smaller than the fabrics covering it. This will not make any difference. The important thing is that the string block is the correct size.

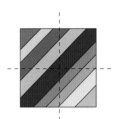

10. Make several string blocks and sew them together in groups of four.

Tip: Sewing four 6-1/2" string blocks together will make a 12" finished block.

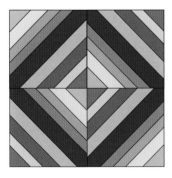

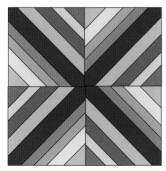

FRAMING THE STRING BLOCKS

1. Create a fun frame by cutting a string block into four string squares.

2. Cut four 3-1/4" x 12-1/2" strips. Attach the string squares to opposite ends of two of the strips. Press seams toward the frame strips. Attach the remaining two strips to opposite sides of the string block. Press seams toward the strips. Sew on the remaining strips. Press seams toward the strips.

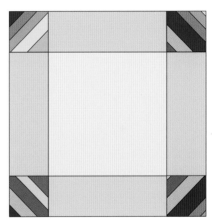

ADDING A LABEL

Labeling your quilt when it is completed is extremely satisfying. Even if the label only includes your name and the date, it is a record of your work that will be valuable to future generations. If the quilt is a gift, you may want to include a message on the label.

Labels on antique quilts give us a glimpse into the lives of the women who made them. If the maker's name is on the quilt, or even just their initials, it gives us something tangible to relate to and connect with. Labeling our quilts assures us that our achievements won't be lost over time and they won't be attributed to the efforts of 'anonymous.' After all, she's already made her fair share of quilts.

There are numerous ways to label your quilts. A few of my favorites are listed.

Permanent marking pen

Permanent marking pens can be found in most sewing and craft stores. These pens have fine tips and come in a wide variety of colors. Write directly on the cotton fabric you are using as a label before appliquéing it to the back of your quilt. If the fabric shifts, making it difficult to write, lay it on a piece of sandpaper. The grit of the sandpaper will stabilize the fabric. You can also iron the fabric to the shiny side of freezer paper, write your message and peel the label off before applying it to the quilt.

Many fabric manufacturers print panels of labels. A blank area is provided where you can write a message as well as your name and the date. (**a**).

a

Embroidery and cross-stitch

Hand embroider your label. You can also machine stitch a label using one of the decorative stitches on your machine. If you are stitching your own label, make sure the label and quilt fabric are similar in weight and weave.

Quilting

A subtle way to make your permanent mark on the quilt is to incorporate your name and the date into the quilting. (**b**)

b

Purchased woven labels

There are a wide range of woven labels available for purchase. These can be personalized and sewn on when you add the binding or appliquéd to the back of the quilt. (**c** and **d**)) I use Cash's woven labels as they are a familiar name from my schooldays.

c

d

Computer-printed label

You can also design your own label on the computer and print it onto specially-prepared fabric sheets. Trim the label and appliqué it to your quilt. This technique allows you to include photos and graphics on the label. (**e**).

Quilt sewn by Carolyn Forster 2005
Includes fabric brought by Mary O'Riordan at Houston Quilt Market, October 2003

e

Laundering

I prefer to wash my quilt before I use it to freshen it up and get rid of any remaining markings. Also, due to the type of batting I use the quilt shrinks slightly embedding the quilting into the fabric, giving it a more textured look.

I wash my quilts in the washing machine on a gentle, cool cycle and dry them on a line outside. If you are worried about surplus dye running into light areas of the quilt use a color or dye catcher. These can be found in most grocery stores. Always remember to test any fabrics that you are concerned may bleed.

THE BLOCKS

A WORD BEFORE YOU START ...

- Before starting on any of the projects in the book please read ALL of the instructions for that project from start to finish.

- Fabric requirements for each project are given in metric and yardage. The unit of measurement for the patchwork in this book is inches.

- The yardage given for the quilts is based on 44"-wide fabric with a usable width of 40".

- The fabric quantities given for each project are the amount of fabric used for the actual design.

When you're buying fabric you might want to add 10-20 percent to allow any shrinkage in pre-washing, any little bits of fabric lost when you're neatening the fabric for rotary cutting, and any little mistakes you might make while cutting or sewing.

- If the block you're going to sew is new to you, it's always worth making a trial one first from scrap fabric. This way you can sort out any issues without worrying about wasting the 'real' fabric for the actual quilt.

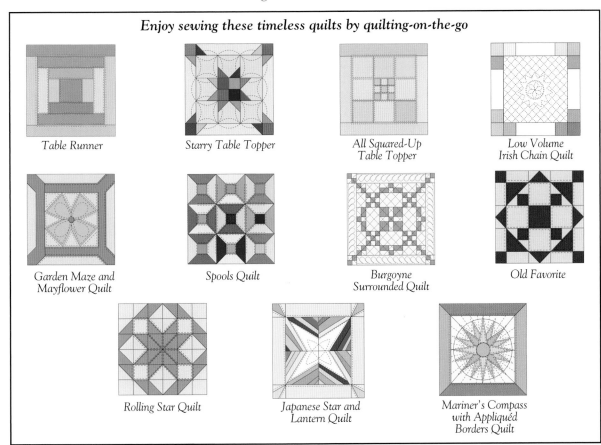

Enjoy sewing these timeless quilts by quilting-on-the-go

Table Runner

Starry Table Topper

All Squared-Up Table Topper

Low Volume Irish Chain Quilt

Garden Maze and Mayflower Quilt

Spools Quilt

Burgoyne Surrounded Quilt

Old Favorite

Rolling Star Quilt

Japanese Star and Lantern Quilt

Mariner's Compass with Appliquéd Borders Quilt

The Projects

Table Runner

Finished framed block size: 16"   Finished runner size: 16½" x 48½"

Ease into the Quilting-on-the-Go process by sewing this simple and speedy runner. With only three blocks to join and no rows to worry about, it is a great beginner project. Pre-cut Jelly Rolls and Charm Squares make it extra speedy to sew, giving you time to enjoy the quilting.

Fabric Requirements

Three 5" (15cm) Charm Squares for center squares
Four or five light-color Jelly Roll strips OR
    2½" x width of fabric strips OR
    15" (35cm) x width of fabric piece
Six or seven dark-color Jelly Roll strips OR
    2½" x width of fabric strips OR
    20" (50cm) x width of fabric piece
1⅛ yards (1m) backing fabric
Three 19" (48cm) squares batting
⅓ yard (25cm) binding fabric

Cutting

From center square fabric, cut: 3—4½" squares
From light-color Jelly Roll strips, cut:
    6—2½" x 4½" strips
    6—2½" x 8½" strips
    6—2½" x 12½" strips
From dark-color Jelly Roll strips, cut:
    6—2½" x 8½" strips
    6—2½" x 12½" strips
    6—2½" x 16½" strips
From backing fabric, cut:
    3—19" squares
From binding, cut:
    4—2½" x length of fabric strips

Method

Making the Blocks

1. Sew 2—2½" x 4½" light-color strips to opposite sides of a center square. Press seams toward the strips.

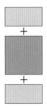

2. Sew 2—2½" x 8½" dark-color strips to the remaining sides of the center square. Press seams toward the strips.

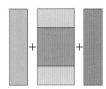

3. Sew 2—2½" x 8½" light-color strips to the top and bottom of the block as shown. Press seams toward strips. Sew 2½" x 12½" dark-color strips to the remaining sides of the block. Press seams toward strips.

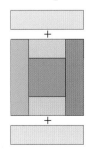
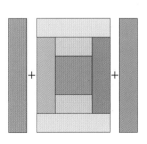

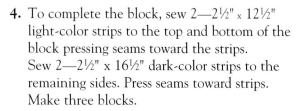

4. To complete the block, sew 2—2½" x 12½" light-color strips to the top and bottom of the block pressing seams toward the strips. Sew 2—2½" x 16½" dark-color strips to the remaining sides. Press seams toward strips. Make three blocks.

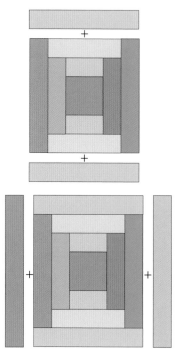

Quilting the Blocks

1. Layer each block with backing and batting. Baste the layers together.

2. Outline quilt ¼" from the seams with a big stitch. Refer to the diagram to see where to stop quilting.

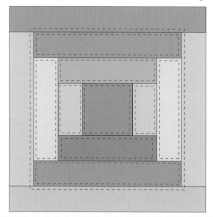

Finishing the Table Runner

1. Lay out the blocks, choosing one of the design options shown.

Referring to page 47, sew the blocks together and quilt the sashing.

3. When the quilting is complete, sew the binding strips together on the diagonal to make one long continuous strip. Press the strip, wrong sides together, along the length. Sew the binding to the quilt referring to page 52. Add a label.

Table Runner

Runner Size: 16½" x 48½"

Starry Table Topper

Finished framed block size: 16" Finished topper size: 32½" x 48½"

Whether you use this little quilt as a table topper or crib quilt, the stars will sparkle. A combination of Hidden Stars frames and easy-to-sew star blocks makes this a great project to practice your Quilting-on-the-Go skills. Wherever you happen to be taking your project the big stitches in the quilting will work up quickly.

Fabric Requirements

1½ yards (1.4m) white muslin or calico
⅔ yard (60cm) fabric for stars OR
   144 pre-cut mini charms OR
   6 Jelly Roll strips
1⅝ yards (1.5m) backing fabric
Six 19" (48cm) squares of batting
⅜ yard (35cm) binding fabric

Cutting

From white muslin or calico, cut:
   48—4½" squares
   24—2½" x 12½" rectangles
From star fabric, cut:
   144—2½" squares
From backing fabric, cut:
   6—19" squares
From binding fabric, cut:
   5—2½" x length of fabric strips

Method

Making the Blocks

1. Draw a diagonal line, corner to corner, on the wrong side of 96—2½" squares.

2. Place a marked 2½" square on the corner of a 4½" muslin square, right sides together. Sew on the drawn line.
   Note: If you choose not to sew directly on the line, sew to the right of it not the left. This way you will not lose fabric when the square is trimmed and pressed into position.

3. Repeat with the remaining 4½" muslin squares. Trim the extra fabric as shown, leaving a ¼" seam allowance. Press seam allowance toward the 4½" square.
   Tip: Chain piecing the squares will save time.

4. Repeat steps 2-3 on an adjacent corner of the 4½" squares.

5. Sew four unmarked 2½" squares together as shown to make a four-patch unit. Press the seams open. Make 6 four-patch units.

Make 6

6. Lay out 4 plain muslin squares, 1 four-patch unit and 4 pieced muslin squares as shown. Sew the pieces together in 3 rows, pressing as indicated by the arrows.

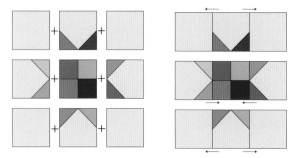

7. Sew the 3 rows together, pressing the seams toward the outside of the block. Make 6 blocks.

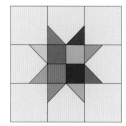

Make 6

Making the Frames

Note: Carefully watch the placement of the triangles as you are sewing.

1. Draw a diagonal line, corner to corner, on the wrong side of 48—2½" squares.

2. Place marked 2½" squares on opposite ends of a 2½" x 12½" muslin rectangle, right sides together. Sew on the drawn line. Trim the extra fabric, leaving a ¼" seam allowance. Press seams open. Make 24 short framing units.

3. Sew a 2½" square to opposite ends of 12 short framing units made in step 2. Press seams open to make 12 long framing units.

4. Sew two short framing units to opposite sides the blocks. Press the seams open.

5. Sew two long framing units to the remaining sides of the blocks. Press the seams open.

Quilting the Blocks

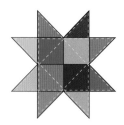

1. Quilt the stars in the center of the block with an outline stitch. The design is worked as a continuous line for ease.

2. Position the Starry Top Circle Template on top of the block and frames and draw lines as shown. Leave approximately 2" from the raw edge of framed block to leave enough space to sew blocks together.

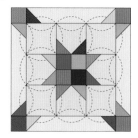

Finishing the Table Topper

1. Referring to page 47, sew the blocks together in pairs to form rows. Use the Starry Top Circle Template to draw lines to span the joined frames. Continue quilting the frames between the blocks.

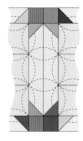

2. Referring to page 51, sew the rows together. Use the Starry Top Circle Template to draw lines to span the joined frames, and complete the quilting.

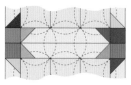

3. Sew the binding strips together on the diagonal to make one long continuous strip. Press the strip, wrong sides together, along the length. Sew the binding to the quilt referring to page 52. Add a label.

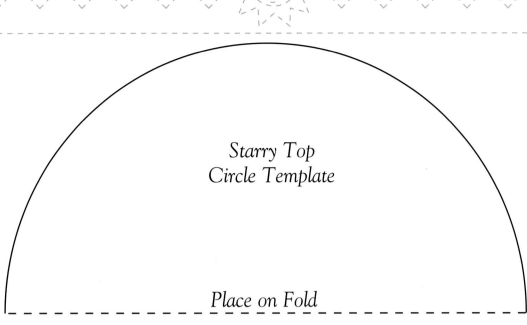

Starry Top
Circle Template

Place on Fold

Starry Top Topper

Table Topper Size: 32½" x 48½"

All Squared-Up Table Topper

Finished framed block size: 16" Finished table topper size: 32½" x 32½"

Using assorted cream fabrics that blend together make this project very forgiving if your stitching is not quite accurate yet. The four blocks are stitched together in two rows, providing a great introduction to the complete quilting-on-the-go process. Two block size choices are given with one using popular pre-cuts.

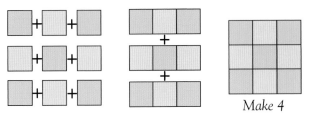

Fabric Requirements

16" finished framed blocks

36—2" Mini Charm Squares in assorted cream prints
32—5" Charm Squares in assorted cream prints
6 Jelly Roll strips in assorted cream prints
1⅛ yards (1m) backing fabic
4—19" (48cm) squares batting
⅓ yard (25cm) binding fabric

Cutting

From assorted cream print Mini Charm Squares, cut:
  36—scant 1⅞" squares
From assorted cream print Charm Squares, cut:
  32—4½" squares
From assorted cream print Jelly Roll strips, cut:
  8—2½" x 12½" rectangles
  8—2½" x 16½" rectangles
From backing fabric, cut:
  4—19" squares
From binding fabric, cut:
  4—2½" x length of fabric strips.

Optional 17½" finished framed blocks

Note: The backing and batting sizes given may still be used. Cut carefully as you will have less room for error.

Cutting

From assorted cream prints, cut:
  36—2" squares
  32—5" squares
  8—2½" x 14" rectangles
  8—2½" x 18" rectangles

Method

Making the Blocks

1. Sew 9 small (1⅞" or 2") squares together in 3 rows with 3 squares in each row as shown. Press seams open. Sew the 3 rows together to make a nine-patch block. Make 4 nine-patch blocks.

Make 4

2. Lay out 8 medium (4½" or 5") squares and 1 nine-patch block as shown. Sew the pieces together in rows, pressing in the direction of the arrows. Sew the rows together to make a nine-patch block, pressing in the direction of the arrows. Make 4 nine-patch blocks.

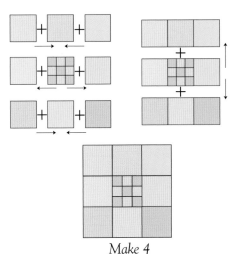

Make 4

Adding the frames

1. Sew 2 shorter rectangles to opposite sides of a nine-patch block. Press the seams toward the rectangles.

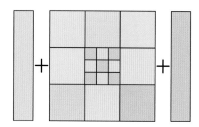

2. Sew 2 longer rectangles to the remaining sides of the nine-patch block. Press the seams toward the rectangles.

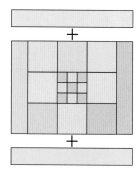

3. Repeat with the remaining 3 nine-patch blocks.

Quilting the blocks

1. Layer the nine-patch blocks, batting and backing together. Baste the pieces together.

2. Quilt the blocks as shown.

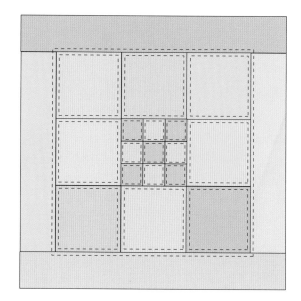

Completing the Quilt

1. Lay out the 4 quilted nine-patch blocks in 2 rows with 2 blocks in each row. The direction of the frames alternate, so there is no need to line up the seams. Sew the blocks together in rows referring to page 47.

2. Sew the rows together referring to page 51.

3. After the sashing is created, outline quilt ¼" from the seams.

4. When the quilting is complete, sew the binding strips together on the diagonal to make one long continuous strip. Press the strip, wrong sides together, along the length. Sew the binding to the quilt referring to page 52. Add a label.

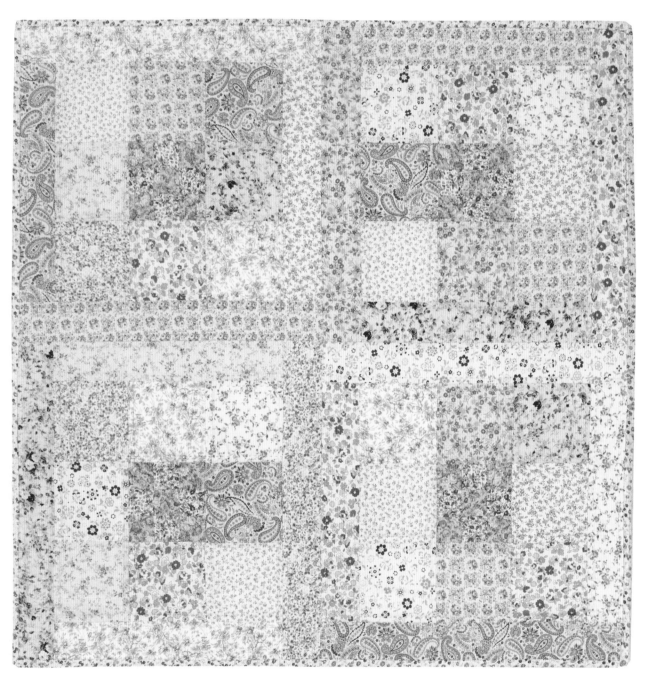

All Squared-Up Table Topper

Table Topper Size: 32½" x 32½"

Low Volume Irish Chain Quilt

Finished block size: 14" Finished quilt size: 70" x 70"

The Irish Chain quilt is wonderful to quilt in small sections. It is slightly different than the other projects in this book as it is made with two different blocks.

The blocks in this quilt have natural frames so no extra planning for adding frames was needed. Keep in mind however that you are sewing two similar sets of blocks for one quilt. To easily identify my blocks I decided to use different backings for Blocks A and B, thus creating a checkerboard quilt back.

Fabric Requirements

$1\frac{3}{4}$ yards (1.6m) White fabric/muslin
$3\frac{3}{8}$ yards (3m) Assorted Scraps
$5\frac{5}{8}$ yards (5.25m) Backing fabric
$\frac{5}{8}$ yard (55cm) Binding fabric
26—16" (40cm) Batting squares

Cutting

From White fabric/muslin, cut:
 12—$10\frac{1}{2}$" squares
 48—$2\frac{1}{2}$" x $6\frac{1}{2}$" rectangles
 52—$2\frac{1}{2}$" squares

From Assorted Scraps, cut:
 144—$2\frac{1}{2}$" squares for Block A
 585—$2\frac{1}{2}$" squares for Block B

From backing fabric, cut:
 25—16" (40 cm) squares

Note: If you don't mind piecing fabric for the backing squares, you will find that for every four squares cut from a width of fabric you will be able to make an extra one from the spare fabric. If you decide to do this you will only need $4\frac{1}{2}$ yards (4.1m) of fabric.

If you choose to use two different fabrics for the backing, you will need $2\frac{3}{4}$ yards (2.5m) for Block A (or $2\frac{3}{8}$ yards (2.1m) if you are joining spare fabric) and $3\frac{1}{4}$ yards 2.9m) for Block B (or $2\frac{3}{4}$ yards (2.5m) if you are joining spare fabric).

From binding fabric, cut:
 8—$2\frac{1}{2}$" x length of fabric strips.

Method

Making the Blocks

Note: All seams are pressed open.

Block A

1. Sew a $2\frac{1}{2}$" scrap square to each end of 4—$2\frac{1}{2}$" x $6\frac{1}{2}$" rectangles. Press seams open.

Make 4

2. Sew an additional $2\frac{1}{2}$" scrap square to each end of 2 of the rectangle units from step 1. Press seams open.

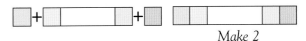

Make 2

3. Sew the short rectangle/square units to opposite sides of a $10\frac{1}{2}$" white/muslin square. Press seams open.

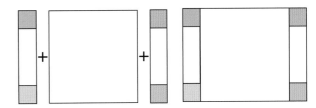

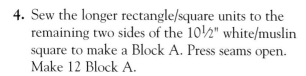

4. Sew the longer rectangle/square units to the remaining two sides of the 10½" white/muslin square to make a Block A. Press seams open. Make 12 Block A.

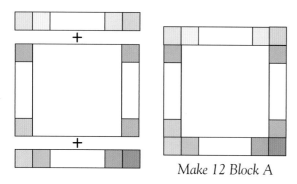

Make 12 Block A

Note: You may trace the Sunflower quilting pattern on page 78 onto the calico square now, or make a template and draw it on after the block is layered with batting and backing fabric. Mark grid lines as shown.

5. Layer Block A, batting and backing together. Baste the pieces together and quilt as shown.

Note: When quilting the grid you can leave threads trailing as necessary. Pick them up again when quilting the blocks that have been joined together. This also applies when quilting Block B.

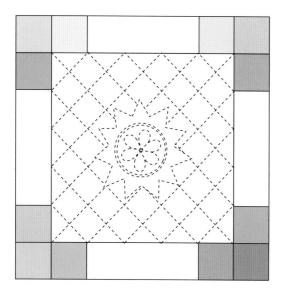

Block B

Note: It is important to use a good selection of fabrics so you won't have too many repeats.

1. Sew 3—2½" scrap squares together to make strip set A. Press all seams open. Make 4 strip set A.

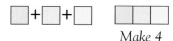

Make 4

2. Sew 5—2½" scrap squares together to make strip set B. Press all seams open. Make 1 strip set B.

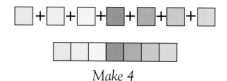

Make 1

3. Sew 7—2½" scrap squares together to make strip set C. Press all seams open. Make 4 strip set C.

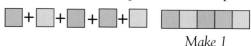

Make 4

4. Sew a 2½" white/calico square to opposite ends of strip set B.

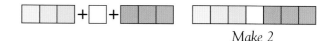

Make 1

5. Sew a 2½" white/calico square to the end of one strip set A. Sew another strip set A to the opposite side of the white/calico square. Repeat with the remaining 2 strip set A.

Make 2

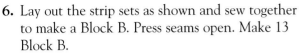

6. Lay out the strip sets as shown and sew together to make a Block B. Press seams open. Make 13 Block B.

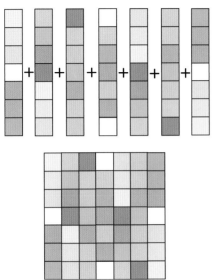

Make 13 Block B

7. Layer Block B, batting and backing together. Baste the pieces together. Mark the quilting lines using the grid of the squares as your guide. I used a Hera Marker for marking the lines. Quilt as shown.

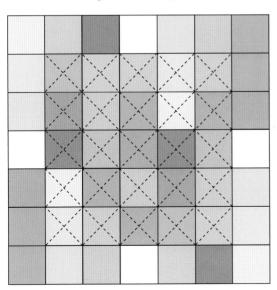

Completing the Quilt

1. Beginning with Block B in the upper right hand corner, lay out the quilted blocks in a checkerboard pattern. You will have five rows of five blocks. Sew the blocks together in rows referring to page 47. Sew the rows together referring to page 51.

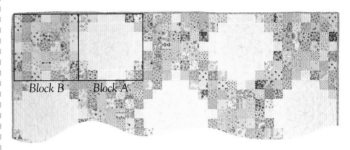

Block B   Block A

2. If you left trailing threads, join the quilting lines with these threads as blocks and rows are joined. If you chose not to leave threads, simply finish quilt lines with new thread.

3. Sew the binding strips together on the diagonal to make one long continuous strip. Press the strip, wrong sides together, along the length.

4. Sew the binding to the quilt referring to page 52. Add a label.

Enlarge templates 105%

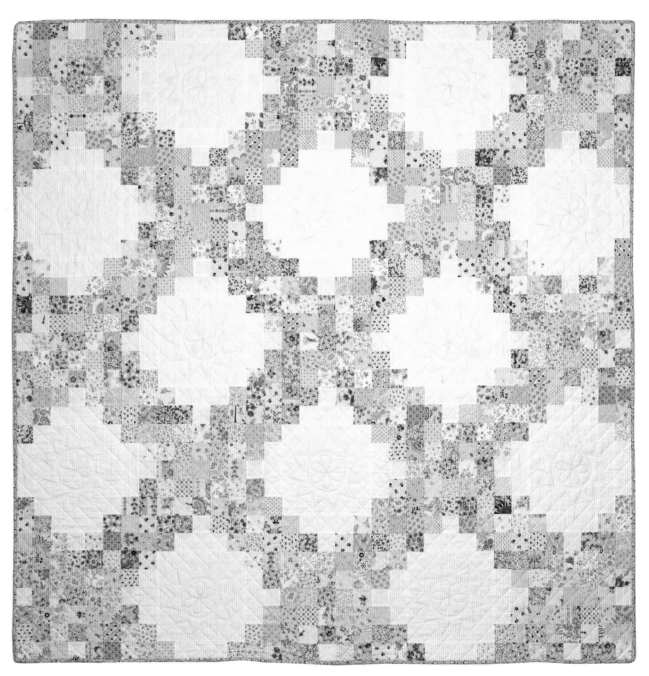

Low Volume Irish Chain Quilt

Quilt Size: 70" x 70"

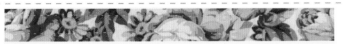

Garden Maze and Mayflower Quilt

Finished block size: 12" Finished quilt size: 48"x 48"

Add a touch of spring to your quilting by sewing your very own flower garden. Nine blocks make a quick and easy project to brighten the back of a sofa, or take it out to the garden for a picnic.

Fabric Requirements

1⅛ yards (1.1m) Background fabric for Mayflower blocks

1⅛ yards (1.1m) fabric for flower petals

Note: You need 9 sets of four petals or 36 petals total. If you are using a selection of fabrics, 1—6½" strip or fat quarter will yield 8 petals.

¼ yard (25cm) fabric for the Mayflower block centers

1⅛ yards (1.1m) Background fabric for Garden Maze frames

1 yard (91cm) fabric for Garden Maze lattice

4½ yards (4.11m) Backing fabric

½ yard (46cm) Binding fabric

9—18" (48cm) Batting squares

Cutting

From Background fabric for Mayflower blocks, cut:
  3—4⅞" strips of fabric. Sub cut the strips into 4⅞" squares. Cut the squares in half diagonally to make 36 corner triangles.
  5—4⅞" strips. Use the template on page 84 to cut 36 background triangles.

From flower petal fabric, cut:
  36 petals using the template on page 84

From the Mayflower block center fabric, cut:
  9 flower centers using the template on page 83

From Background fabric for Garden Maze frames, cut:
  36—1½" x 12½" background strips
  72—1½" background squares

From Garden Maze lattice fabric, cut:
  36—1½" x 12½" lattice strips
  36—2½" lattice squares

From backing fabric, cut:
  9—18" squares

From binding fabric, cut:
  6—2½" x length of fabric strips

Method

Making the Mayflower Blocks

1. For ease of piecing, lightly mark a dot on points of petals and background triangles as indicated on templates on page 84. Separate the flower petals into 9 sets with 4 petals in each set. Layer 2 petals, right sides together. Referring to the diagram, stitch along one short edge stopping ¼" from where the petals form a "Y". Press the seams open. Repeat with another pair of petals.

2. Layer the pairs of petals, right sides together, matching the seams. Sew the pairs together, starting and stopping ¼" from each of the raw edges. Press the seam open.

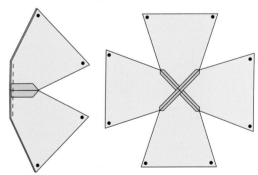

3. With right sides together, match the marked point and raw edge of a triangle to a point and raw edge of a flower petal. With the petal on top of the triangle, stitch toward the flower center, stopping at the ¼" opening where petals are joined. Backstitch to secure seam end. Match the

marked point and raw edge of triangle to adjacent petal. Sew from center to outer edge of petal. Press seams toward petals. Repeat with the remaining triangles.

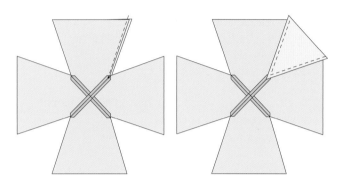

4. With flower unit wrong side up, fold in half and in half again, finger pressing creases into each outside edge of the flower petals. Fold 4 triangles in half and finger press. Match creases on the triangles to those on the flower petals and stitch in place. Press seams toward the corner triangles.

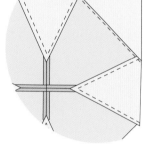

5. Using your favorite appliqué method, appliqué a flower center on the block to complete a Mayflower block. Make 9 Mayflower blocks.

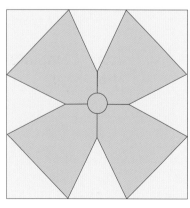

Make 9

Making the Garden Maze Frames

1. Layer a 1½" x 12½" lattice strip and a 1½" x 12½" background strip, right sides together. Sew the strips together along one long edge. Press the seam toward the lattice fabric. Make 36 lattice strip sets.

Make 36

2. Draw a diagonal line from corner to corner on the wrong side of the 1½" background squares.

3. Referring to the diagram and with right sides together, place two marked squares on opposite corners of a 2½" lattice square. Sew along the drawn lines. Trim a ¼" from the stitched lines. Press seams open to complete a lattice square. Make 36 lattice squares.

Make 36

4. Sew lattice squares to opposite ends of 18 lattice strip sets. Press seams open.

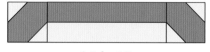

Make 18

Finishing the Mayflower Block

1. Sew lattice strip sets without the lattice squares to opposite sides of a Mayflower blocks. Press seams open.

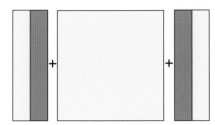

2. Sew the lattice strip sets with the lattice squares to the remaining sides of the Mayflower block. Press seams open. Make 9 Mayflower blocks.

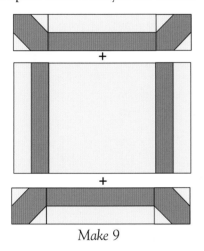

Make 9

3. Quilt the blocks as shown. Quilt in the ditch around the flower center and use the petal template to quilt inside the petals. Outline quilt ¼" from the seams of the block pieces and into the frame.

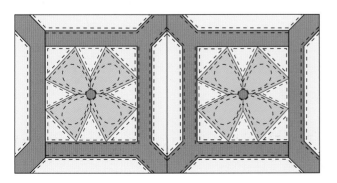

Completing the Quilt

1. Lay out the quilted blocks in three rows with three blocks in each row. Sew the blocks together referring to page 47.

2. Fill in the remaining quilting as the blocks are sewn together. Outline quilt ¼" from the seams.

3. Sew the rows together referring to page 51.

3. Sew the binding strips together on the diagonal to make one long continuous strip. Press the strip, wrong sides together, along the length.

4. Sew the binding to the quilt referring to page 52. Add a label.

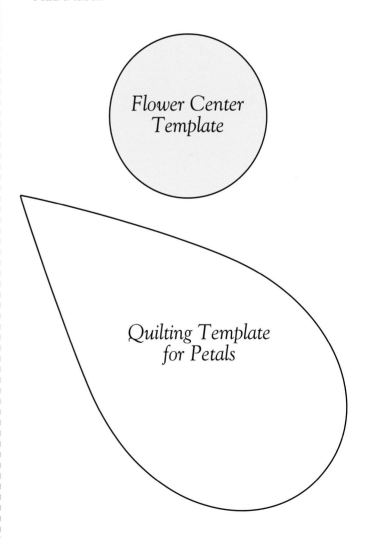

Flower Center Template

Quilting Template for Petals

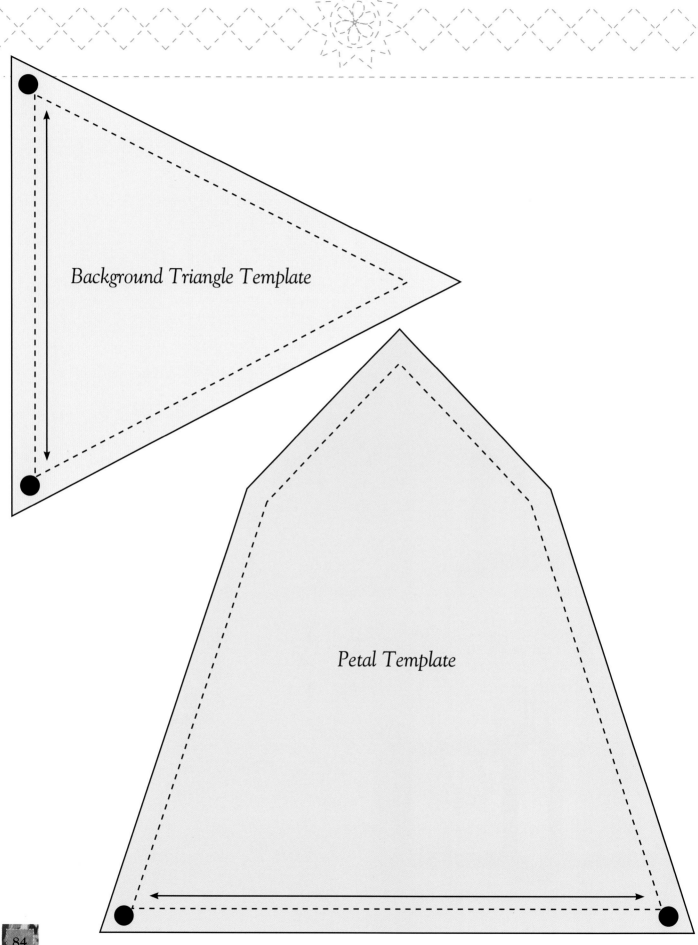

Background Triangle Template

Petal Template

Garden Maze and Mayflower Quilt

Quilt Size: 48" x 48"

Spools Quilt

Finished individual spool block size: 6" Finished spool unit size: 18" x 18"
Finished quilt size: 72½" x 72½"

This scrappy spools quilt can be made using scraps and leftover pieces of Jelly Roll strips. Refer to page 26 for more ideas on combining small blocks into units that can be sewn using the Quilting-on-the-Go technique.

Fabric Requirements

3¾ yards (3.4m) assorted medium/dark fabric
   for spools
3¾ yards (3.4m) assorted light fabric for spools
⅔ yard (60cm) assorted fabric for spool centers
4½ yards (4.1m) backing fabric
16—20" (50cm) squares of batting
⅝ yard (57cm) binding fabric

Cutting

From medium/dark fabric, cut:
   288—2½" x 7¼" rectangles
From light fabric, cut:
   288—2½" x 7¼" rectangles
From assorted fabric for spool centers, cut:
   144—2½" squares
From backing fabric, cut:
   16—20" squares
From binding fabric, cut:
   8—2½" x length of fabric strips

Method

Making the Spool Blocks

1. Using the 45-degree angle on a rotary cutting ruler, trim the corners of the 2½" x 7¼" rectangles.

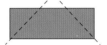

2. Sew a medium/dark trimmed rectangle to opposite sides of a 2½" spool center square. Stitch the pieces right sides together with the center square on top. Begin and end stitching ¼" from the edge. Press seams open.

3. Layer the light trimmed rectangle and the sewn medium/dark trimmed rectangle, right sides together, with points aligned and the medium/dark trimmed rectangle on top.

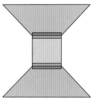

4. Sew from the point to the open seam. Leaving the needle in the work, lift the presser foot and pivot the center of the spool block so it aligns with the edge of the light trimmed rectangle underneath. Lower the presser foot and stitch to the next open seam.

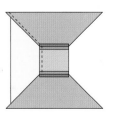

5. Repeat the process, stitching down the remaining side of the spool.

6. In the same manner, stitch a light trimmed rectangle to the opposite side of the spool. Press the seams toward the center. Make 144 spool blocks.

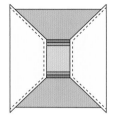

Making the Spool Units

1. Referring to the diagram for placement, lay out 9 spool blocks in 3 rows with 3 blocks in each row.

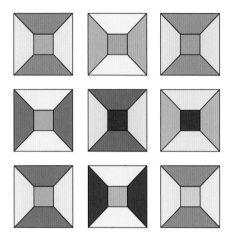

2. Sew the blocks together in rows using the arrows as a pressing guide. Pressing the seams in opposite directions will help the blocks lay flat.

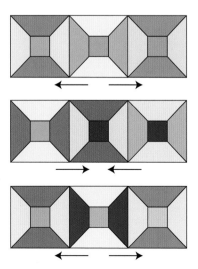

3. Sew the rows together to make a spool block unit. Make 16 spool units.

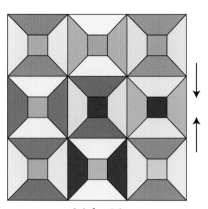

Make 16

Quilting the Spool Block Units

Layer the spool block unit, batting, and backing. Baste the pieces together. I outline quilted the blocks ¼" from the seam allowance using a big stitch Perle cotton (no. 12) thread. Quilt the block units as shown, leaving about 2" free of stitching around raw edges of block. Leave trailing threads so they can be rethreaded to continue quilting when the units are joined together.

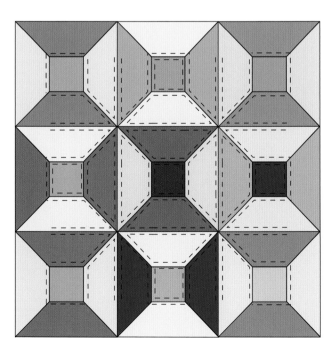

Completing the Quilt

1. Lay out the quilted blocks in 4 rows with 4 blocks in each row. Sew the blocks together in rows referring to page 51. As the blocks are sewn together, join the quilting lines using the trailing threads. Stitch the rows in the same manner.

2. Sew the binding strips together on the diagonal to make one long continuous strip. Press the strip, wrong sides together, along the length. Sew the binding to the quilt referring to page 52. Add a label.

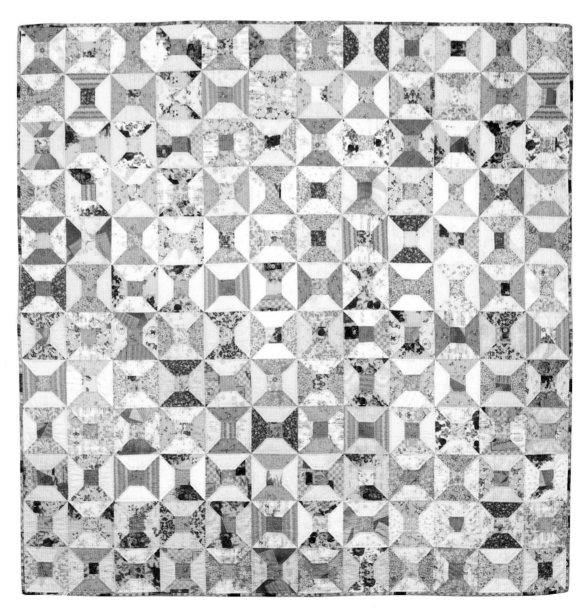

Spools Quilt
Quilt Size: 72½" x 72½"

Burgoyne Surrounded Quilt

Finished block size: 25½"   Finished quilt size: 75½" x 75½"

This classic quilt lends itself wonderfully to the quilting-on-the-go technique. The blocks have the frames 'built-in' so there is no extra planning or decisions to make, plus you only need nine blocks for this fabulous quilt. Since this quilt is so large, it it helpful to work on it in manageable pieces. However, each framed block is 25½" square which is the largest size block I would quilt in a quilting-on-the-go project. If the units get any larger you are nearly back to quilting a regular size quilt.

The quilting on Burgoyne Surrounded was inspired by an antique quilt seen in the book Burgoyne Surrounded by Elizabeth Hamby Carlson, (TPP 2004).

Fabric Requirements

6⅝ yards (6m) light fabric
3¼ yards (3m) dark fabric
6¾ yards (6.25m) backing fabric
9—27" (68cm) square pieces batting
⅝ yard (55cm) dark fabric for binding
  Note: I used only one dark fabric in the quilt for continuity.

Cutting

From light fabric, cut:
    18—2" x width of fabric strips
    3—3½" x width of fabric strips
    36—3½" x 23" strips for frames
    72—3½" x 5" rectangles for background
    36—5" x 8" rectangles for background
From dark fabric, cut:
    17—2" x width of fabric strips
    4—3½" x width of fabric strips
From backing fabric, cut:
    9—27" squares
From binding fabric, cut:
    8—2½" x length of fabric strips

Method

Making the Blocks

1. Sew 3½" x width of fabric light strips to opposite sides of a 2" x width of fabric dark strip to make a strip set. Press seams toward the dark strip. Make 3 strip sets. Subcut the strip sets into 45—2" A units.

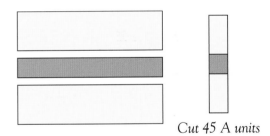

Cut 45 A units

2. Sew 3½" x width of fabric dark strips to opposite sides of a 2" x width of fabric light strip to make a strip set. Press seams toward the dark strips. Make 2 strip sets. Subcut the strip sets into 36—2" B units.

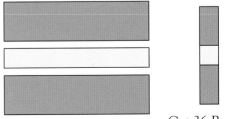

Cut 36 B units

3. Sew 36 A units and 36 B units together as shown to make a C unit. Press seams toward the B unit. Make 36 C units.

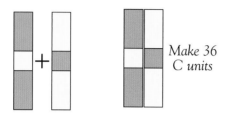

Make 36 C units

4. Sew a 2" x width of fabric dark strip to a 2" x width of fabric light strip to make a strip set. Press seams toward the dark strip. Make 4 strip sets. Subcut the strip sets into 144—2" units.

Cut 144 2" units

5. Sew the 2" units from step 4 into four-patch units as shown. Make 72 four-patch units.

Make 72 four-patch units

6. Sew 2" x width of fabric light strips to opposite sides of a 2" x width of fabric dark strip to make a strip set. Press seams toward dark strip. Make 2 strip sets. Subcut the strip sets into 36—2" D unit.

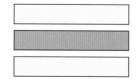

Cut 36 D units

7. Sew 2" x width of fabric dark strips to opposite sides of a 2" x width of fabric light strip to make a strip set. Press seams toward dark strips. Make 4 strip sets. Subcut the strip sets into 72—2" E unit.

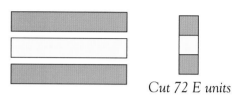

Cut 72 E units

8. Sew 2 E units to opposite sides of a D unit to make a nine-patch unit. Press seams toward the E units. Make 36 nine-patch units.

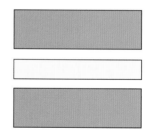
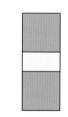

Make 36 nine-patch units

9. Sew 3½" x width of fabric dark strips to opposite sides of a 2" x width of fabric light strip to make a strip set. Press seams toward the dark strips. Make 2 strip sets. Subcut the strip sets into 36—3½" F units.

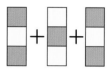

Cut 36 F units

10. Sew 2 F units to opposite sides of an A unit to make a center nine-patch unit. Press seams toward the F units. Make 9 center nine-patch units.

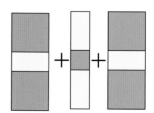
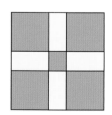

Make 9 center nine-patch units

11. Referring to the diagram, lay out 4 four-patch blocks, 4 nine-patch units, 4 C units, 8—3½ x 5" background rectangles, 4—5" x 8" background rectangles, and 1 center nine-patch unit in rows. Sew the pieces together in rows pressing in the direction indicated by the arrows.

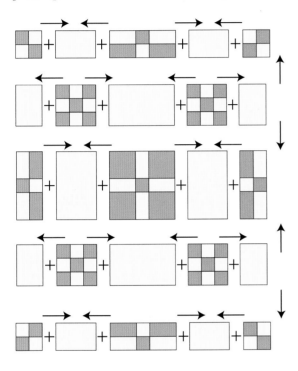

12. Sew the rows together pressing in the direction indicated by the arrows to complete the block. Make 9 blocks.

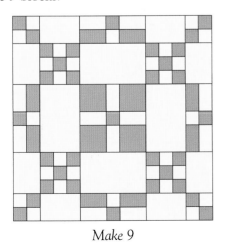

Make 9

Adding the Frames

1. Sew 3½" x 23" strips to opposite sides of the block. Press seams away from the block.

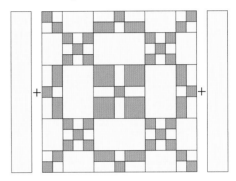

2. Sew four-patch units to opposite ends of 2—3½" x 23" strips. Press seams toward the strips. Sew the pieced strips to the remaining sides of the block, pressing seams away from the block. Repeat with the remaining blocks.

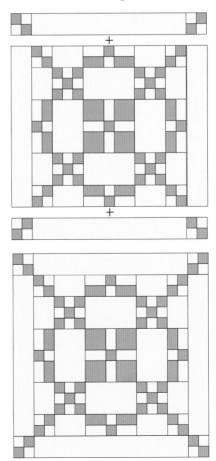

Quilting the Blocks

1. To mark the feather design, draw a line ¾" in from all four raw outside edges of the block. Use the Feather Quilting Template to mark the feathers. Take note of the directions of the feathers so when the blocks are joined the feathers will match.

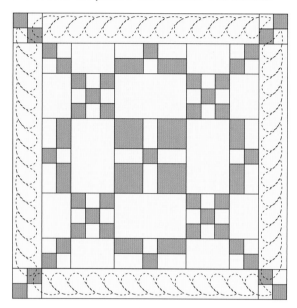

2. Layer the marked block, batting and backing. Baste the pieces together. Mark the diagonal grid with a Hera marker and quilt the layered blocks.

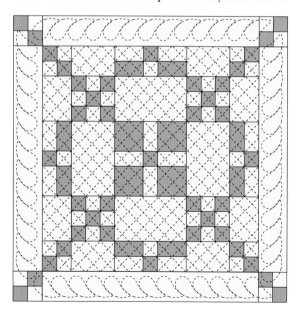

Completing the Quilt

1. Lay out the quilted blocks in 3 rows with 3 blocks in each row. Sew the blocks together in rows referring to page 51. Finish any quilting between the blocks. Stitch the rows together in the same manner.

2. Sew the binding strips together on the diagonal to make one long continuous strip. Press the strip, wrong sides together, along the length. Sew the binding to the quilt referring to page 51. Add a label.

Feather Quilting Template

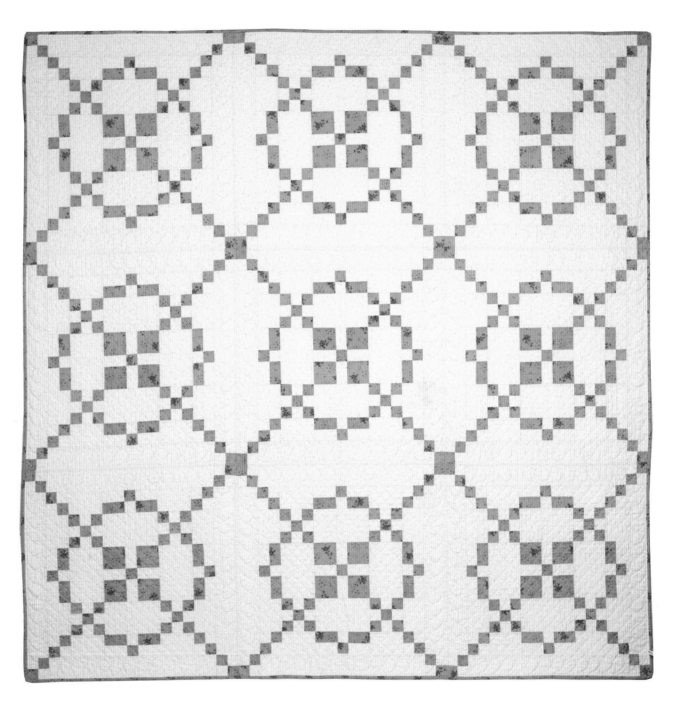

Burgoyne Surrounded Quilt

Quilt Size: 75½" x 75½"

Old Favorite Quilt

Finished block size: 16" Finished quilt size: 64½" x 64½"

This simple but interesting block has frames included. I used one fabric for each block, but it would be fun to sew the print triangles from one fabric and the squares from another for a completely different look.

Fabric Requirements

1⅞ yards (1.7m) assorted print fabrics

Note: If you want to use a different print for each block, you will need 16 fat quarters.

3 yards (2.7m) cream fabric
1⅛ yards (2.8m) backing fabric
16—18" (45cm) squares batting
⅝ yard (50cm) binding fabric

Cutting

From assorted print fabrics, cut:
    16—4½" squares
    128—2½" squares
    32—4⅞" squares. Cut each square in half
    diagonally to make 64 half-square triangles.
    16—5¼" squares. Cut each square in quarters
    diagonally to make 64 quarter-square triangles.

From cream fabric, cut:
    64—4½" squares
    128—2½" x 4½" rectangles
    128—2⅞" squares. Cut each square in half
    diagonally to make 64 half-square triangles.

From backing fabric, cut:
    16—18" squares

From binding fabric, cut:
    7—2½" x length of fabric strips

Method

Making the Blocks

1. Sew cream half-square triangles to adjacent sides of a print 2½" square to make an A unit. Press seams toward the half-square triangles. Make 4 A units.

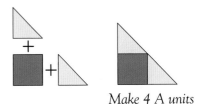

Make 4 A units

2. Sew a print half-square triangle to the A unit to make a B unit. Press seams toward the print half-square triangle. Make 4 B units.

Make 4 B units

3. Sew cream half-square triangles to either side of a print quarter-square triangle to make a C unit. Press seams toward the half-square triangles. Make 4 C units.

Make 4 C units

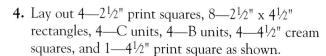

4. Lay out 4—2½" print squares, 8—2½" x 4½" rectangles, 4—C units, 4—B units, 4—4½" cream squares, and 1—4½" print square as shown.

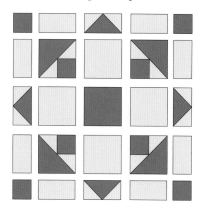

5. Sew the pieces together in rows. Press the seams in the directions indicated by the arrows.

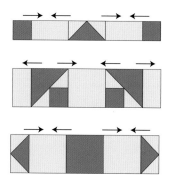

6. Sew the rows together, pressing seams in the direction indicated by the arrows. Make 16 blocks.

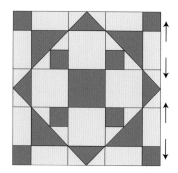

Make 16

Quilting the Blocks

1. Layer the block, batting and backing. Baste the pieces together.

2. Outline quilt the blocks ¼" from the seams referring to the diagram. You could also use the block's grid to mark cross hatching. See the quilting diagram for the Irish Chain Quilt on page 77.

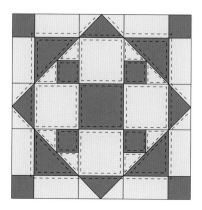

Completing the Quilt

1. Lay out the quilted blocks in 4 rows with 4 blocks in each row. Sew the blocks together in rows referring to page 51. Sew the rows together and finish the quilting referring to the diagram.

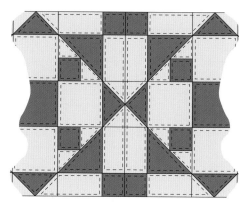

2. Sew the binding strips together on the diagonal to make one long continuous strip. Press the strip, wrong sides together, along the length. Sew the binding to the quilt referring to page 52. Add a label.

Old Favorite Quilt

Quilt Size: 64½" x 64½"

Rolling Star Quilt

Finished block size: 16" Finished quilt size: 64" x 80"

The Rolling Star Quilt was inspired by the quilts of Talula Gilbert Bottoms. I especially liked the Star and Chain quilt, which falls into a group of blocks with natural frames that lend themselves to the Quilting-on-the-Go process. It was an ideal way for me to tackle this quilt in small, bite-size pieces.

Note: My quilt uses set-in seams to make the Rolling Star blocks. I prefer this method because it means fewer seams to quilt through. I have included optional instructions on page 105 if you prefer not to use set-in seams.

Fabric Requirements

3⅔ yards (3.5m) cream background fabric
3⅜ yards (3.1m) assorted print fabrics for stars
20—18" (45cm) squares batting
5 yards (4.5m) backing fabric
½ yard (50cm) binding fabric

Cutting

From the cream background fabric, cut:
    80—3¾" squares
    40—6" squares. Cut each square in quarters
    diagonally to make 160 quarter-square triangles.
    40—5⅝" squares. Cut each square in half
    diagonally to make 80 half-square corner triangles.
From the assorted print fabric for stars, cut:
    320 diamonds using the template on page 104.
    Each block uses 16 diamonds.
       Note: Sixteen diamonds can be cut from 1 Fat
       Quarter or 1—6" x width of fabric strip. Cut strips
       of fabric 3"-wide and use the template on page 104
       to cut the diamonds.
From backing fabric, cut:
    20—18" squares
From binding fabric, cut:
    7—2½" x length of fabric strips.

Method

Making the Blocks

1. Layer 2 diamonds, right sides together. Begin sewing at the narrow point of the diamonds' raw edges. Sew toward the wide angle, stopping ¼" from the raw edge. Take a backstitch. Press seams open to make a diamond pair. Repeat to make 80 diamond pairs.

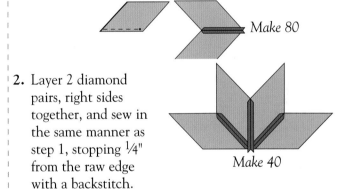

Make 80

2. Layer 2 diamond pairs, right sides together, and sew in the same manner as step 1, stopping ¼" from the raw edge with a backstitch. Press seams open to make a diamond half. Repeat to make 40 diamond halves.

Make 40

3. Layer 2 diamond halves, right sides together. Sew the diamond halves together, starting and stopping ¼" from the raw edges with a backstitch. Press the seam open to make a center star. Make 20 center stars.

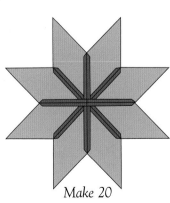

Make 20

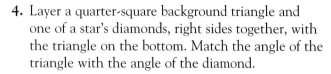

4. Layer a quarter-square background triangle and one of a star's diamonds, right sides together, with the triangle on the bottom. Match the angle of the triangle with the angle of the diamond.

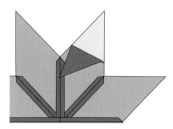

5. Sew from the diamond point to the open seam. Leaving needle in the work, lift the presser foot. Pivot the star so the adjacent side aligns with the remaining side of triangle. Sew to the outside point of star. Press the seams toward the triangle.

   Note: The triangle can be sewn to diamond one seam at a time, ending each seam with a backstitch. Align triangle with next diamond side. Start the stitch from open ¼" seam and sew to point.

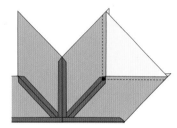

6. Referring to step 5, sew 3 additional quarter-square triangles to the center star.

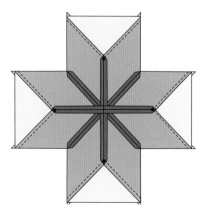

7. Layer the pieced center star from step 6 and a 3¾" background square, right sides together, with the square on the bottom. Match the long raw edge of a diamond with the raw edge of the square. Stitch the pieces together in the same manner used for setting in the quarter-square triangles in step 5. Press the seams toward the diamond.

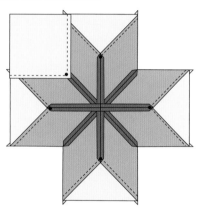

8. Repeat step 7 to sew 3 additional squares to the pieced center star. Make 20 pieced center stars.

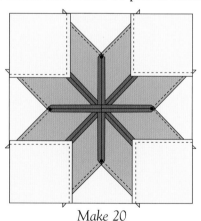

Make 20

Making the Frames

1. Referring to the diagram for placement, layer a diamond on a quarter-square background triangle. Offset the angles as shown to achieve a straight edge. Sew the pieces together pressing the seams toward the diamond.

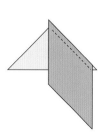

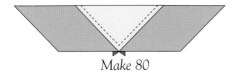

2. Repeat with another diamond on the opposite side of the quarter-square triangle. Press seams toward diamond to make a frame. Make 80 frames.

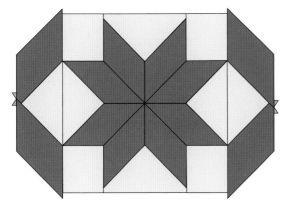

Make 80

Finishing the Blocks

1. Sew frames to opposite sides of a pieced center star. Press the seams open.

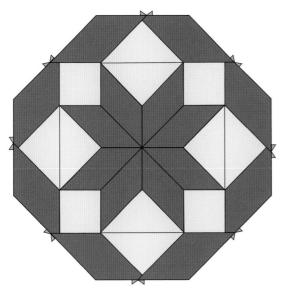

2. Sew frames to the remaining sides of the pieced center star. Press the seams open.

3. Fold a half-square corner triangle in half and finger press. Match the crease to the center of the pieced center star and pin. Sew the pieces together, pressing the seams toward the triangle.

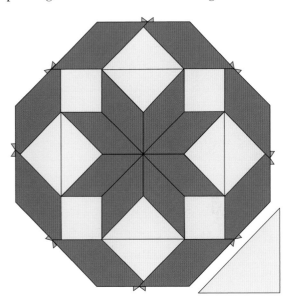

4. Repeat on the 3 remaining corners of the block to make a Rolling Star block. Make 20 Rolling Star blocks.

Make 20

Quilting the Blocks

1. Layer the block, batting and backing. Baste the pieces together.

2. Quilt the blocks as shown in the diagram, taking note of where to stop quilting.

Completing the Quilt

1. Lay out the quilted blocks in 4 rows with five blocks in each row. Sew the blocks together in rows referring to page 51.

2. Sew the rows together. Referring to the diagram, fill in the remaining outline quilting. In the space where four blocks meet use the Diamond Template to make the star.

3. Sew the binding strips together on the diagonal to make one long continuous strip. Press the strip, wrong sides together, along the length. Sew the binding to the quilt referring to page 52. Add a label.

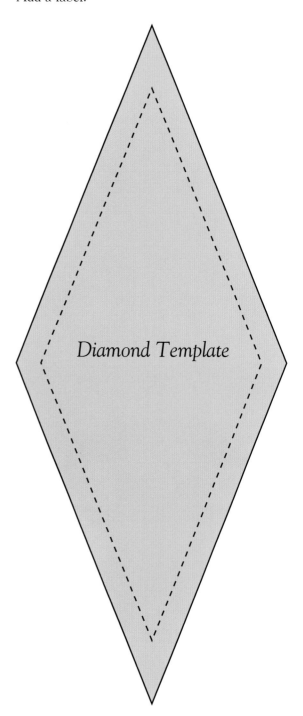

Diamond Template

Rolling Star Quilt without set-in seams

Finished block size: 18"   Finished quilt size: 72½" x 90½"

Read through all instructions before you begin. You may wish to incorporate some of your favorite time-saving cutting and piecing techniques into the project.

Fabric Requirements

5⅞ yards (5.5m) cream background fabric
10 assorted print fat quarters
   or 2½ yards (2.29m) assorted print fabrics for stars
5⅝ yards (5.2m) backing fabric
20—20" (50cm) squares of batting
⅝ yard (60cm) binding fabric

Cutting

From cream background fabric, cut:
   160—3½" squares
   160—3⅞" squares. Cut each square in half
   diagonally to make 320 half-square triangles.
   20—7¼" squares. Cut each square in quarters to
   make 80 quarter-square triangles.
From the assorted print fat quarters or fabrics, cut:
   20—6½" squares
   240—3⅞" squares. Cut each square in half
   diagonally to make 480 half-square triangles.
From the backing fabric, cut:
   20—20" squares
From the binding fabric, cut:
   9—2½" by length of fabric strips

Method

Making the Blocks

1. Sew print half-square triangles to opposite sides of a cream quarter-square triangle as shown. Press seams to dark triangles to make an A unit. Make 4 A units.

Make 4

2. Sew a 3½" cream square to opposite ends of 2 A units. Press seams toward the squares to make a B unit.

Make 2

3. Sew A units to opposite sides of a print 6½" square. Press seams toward the square.

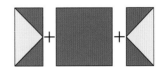

4. Sew B units to the remaining sides of the cream 6½" square. Press seams toward the square to make a center star. Make 20 center stars.

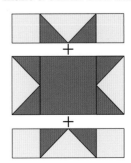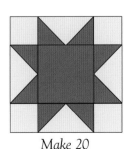

Make 20

Making the Frames

1. Layer a cream half-square triangle and a print half-square triangle, right sides together. Sew the pieces together along the long edge. Press seams open to make a half-square triangle unit. Make 320 half-square triangle units.

 Make 320

2. To make the block frames, sew 4 half-square triangle units together in a row. Refer to the diagram for unit orientation. Press seams open to make a C frame. Make 80 C frames.

Make 80

3. Sew a cream 3½" square to opposite ends of 40 C frames. Press seams open to make a D frame. Make 40 D frames.

Make 40

Finishing the Blocks

1. Sew C frames to opposite sides of the center star. Press seams open.

2. Sew D frames to the remaining sides of the center star. Press seams open to make a Rolling Star block. Make 20 Rolling Star blocks.

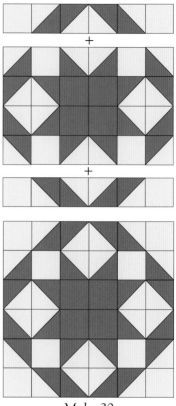

Make 20

Quilting the Blocks

1. Layer the block, batting and backing. Baste the pieces together.

2. Quilt the blocks as shown in the diagram, taking note of where to stop quilting.

106

Completing the Quilt

1. Lay out the quilted blocks in 4 rows with 5 blocks in each row. Sew the blocks together in rows referring to page 47.

2. Sew the rows together referring to page 51. Fill in the remaining outline quilting. In the space where four blocks meet use the Diamond Template on page 104 to make the star.

3. Sew the binding strips together on the diagonal to make one long continuous strip. Press the strip, wrong sides together, along the length. Sew the binding to the quilt referring to page 52. Add a label.

Rolling Star Quilt

Quilt Size with set-in seams: 64" x 80"; Quilt Size without set-in seams: 72½" x 90½"

Japanese Star and Lantern Quilt

Finished block size: 12" Finished quilt size: 48½" x 48½"

Create simple blocks that transform into twinkling stars and lanterns when grouped together. I used fabric pieces left over from other quilts and the strips that were cut off when squaring up my fabrics. The blocks were then sewn together in groups of four and frames were added. In each corner of the frames I stitched a cone shape, so another star is formed when the groups of blocks are put together.

Fabric Requirements

2⅝ yards (2.4m) muslin
¾ yard (75cm) assorted fabrics to outline stars, plus
  additional scraps and strips
9—18" squares of batting
2½ yards (2.5m) backing fabric
½ yard (50cm) binding fabric
¼ yard (25cm) lightweight Pellon (Vilene)
Template material

Cutting

From the muslin, cut:
  36—6½" squares for foundations
  36—2½" x 12½" strips for frames
  72—2" x 4" rectangles
From assorted fabric scraps and strips, cut:
  strips in a variety of widths and lengths
  Note: A variety of fabrics will add interest to the block,
  however to link everything together use the same fabric as
  the first strip on each block and as the binding.
  36—2½" squares for frame corners
From backing fabric, cut:
  9—18" squares
From binding fabric, cut:
  6—2½" x length of fabric strips
From lightweight Pellon (Vilene), cut:
  36—2½" squares
From template material, cut:
  1—Template A
  1—Template B

Method

Making the Blocks

1. Using Template A, align the corner marked X with a corner on the wrong side of a 6½" muslin foundation square. With a pencil or fabric marking tool, trace around the template. Mark the remaining foundation squares in the same manner.

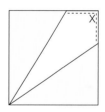

2. Place an assorted fabric strip right side up on a flat surface. Place a marked foundation square right side down on top of the strip. The drawn line will be clearly visible on the foundation square. Align the strip so the majority of fabric is to the left of the drawn line and approximately ¼" to the right. This is the seam allowance.

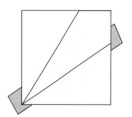

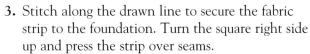

3. Stitch along the drawn line to secure the fabric strip to the foundation. Turn the square right side up and press the strip over seams.

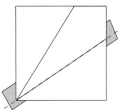

4. In the same manner stitch a fabric strip to the remaining drawn line on the foundation square. Don't worry about any excess fabric hanging over the edge of the square; these will be trimmed off when you finish the block.

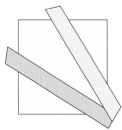

5. Working from the front of the block, match the raw edges of a fabric strip to the raw edge of the recently added strip. Make sure the new strip extends past the foundation square at each end. Using a ¼" seam allowance, stitch through the three fabric layers. Press strip over seam.

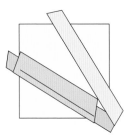
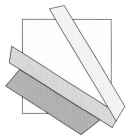

6. Continue to add strips in the same manner until the foundation square is covered. As you near the corners use slightly larger pieces so there will not be too many seam allowances in the corners.

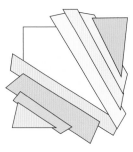

7. Turn the covered foundation square wrong side up and trim the excess fabric in line with the foundation square. The star point unit should measure 6½" square. Make 36 star point units.

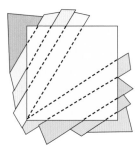
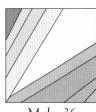

Make 36

8. Layer 2 star point units right sides together. Sew the units together and press the seams open. Repeat with another pair of star point units.

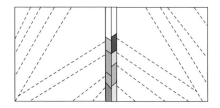

9. Layer the star point unit pairs right sides together. Sew the pairs together, pressing the seams open to make a Star block. Make 9 Star blocks.

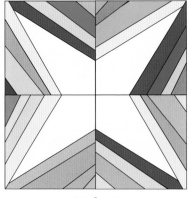

Make 9

Making the Frames

1. Using Template B and the 2½" assorted fabric squares, cut out 36 kite shapes. Place a fabric kite shape, right side up, on a 2½" lightweight Pellon

square matching the wide part of the kite shape with a corner of the Pellon square.

Cut 36

2. Layer a 2½" x 4" rectangle on the kite shape right sides together and with raw edges aligned. Using a ¼" seam allowance stitch along the raw edge securing the fabric to the Pellon.

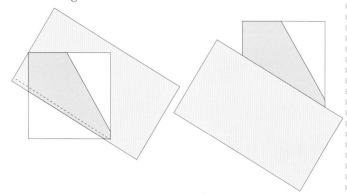

3. Finger-press the muslin away from the kite shape, covering the Pellon. Repeat on the remaining side of the kite shape to make a corner block. Trim the block to 2½". Make 36 corner blocks.

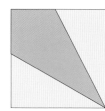

Make 36

4. Sew corner blocks to opposite ends of a 2½" x 12½" muslin strip. Press seams open to make a long frame. Make 18 long frames.

Make 18

Finishing the Blocks

1. Sew a 2½" x 12½" muslin strip to opposite sides of a Star block. Press the seams open.

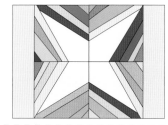

2. Sew a long frame to the remaining sides of a Star block. Press the seams open to make a framed Star block. Make 9 framed Star blocks.

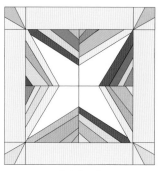

Make 9

Quilting the Blocks

1. Layer the block, batting and backing. Baste the pieces together.

2. Quilt the blocks as shown in the diagram, taking note of where to stop quilting.

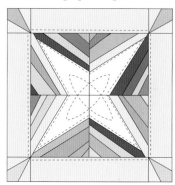

Completing the Quilt

1. Lay out the quilted blocks in 3 rows with 3 blocks in each row. Sew the blocks together in rows referring to page 47.

2. Sew the rows together referring to page 51. Fill in the remaining outline quilting.

3. Sew the binding strips together on the diagonal to make one long continuous strip. Press the strip, wrong sides together, along the length. Sew the binding to the quilt referring to page 52. Add a label.

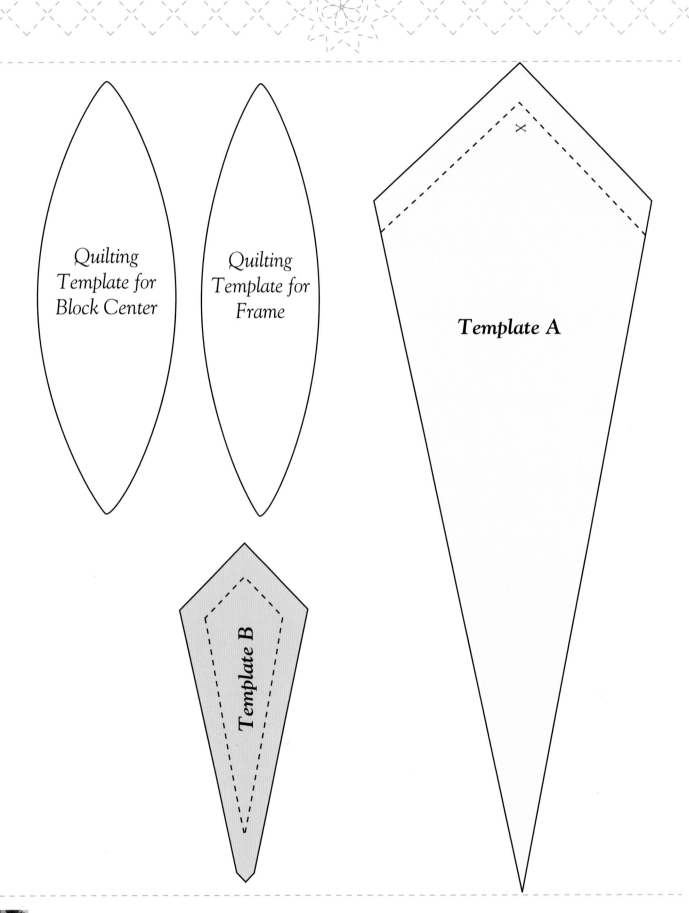

Quilting
Template for
Block Center

Quilting
Template for
Frame

Template A

Template B

Japanese Star and Lantern Quilt

Quilt Size: 47" x 47"

Mariner's Compass with Appliqué Borders

Finished framed block size: 16" Finished quilt size: 80" x 80"

I have always loved the mariner's compass block. The Quilting-on-the-Go technique was a great chance to stitch a quilt in small manageable pieces and then add a border. I admire the appliqué borders on older quilts where the maker didn't worry about continuing the design around the corners. This made it easy for me to incorporate into my quilt. Although the vine is the same on all four sides, I used different flower and leaf motifs on each side to add interest to the quilt. If you prefer not to do the appliqué, use a print fabric. Borders can be added to any quilting-on-the-go project.

Fabric Requirements

2¾ yards (2.75m) background fabric
Note: I used the same fabric for the background and the border. If you plan to do this add the background and border yardages together.

2¼ yards (2.1m) coordinating fabric scraps
for compasses*
   Note: If you are fussy cutting or using directional fabrics you may want to purchase additional fabric.

1⅞ yards (1.8m) border fabric
1½ yards (1.5m) frame A fabric
1½ yards (1.5m) frame B fabric
1½ yards (1.5m) appliqué vine fabric
Assorted scraps for appliqué flowers and leaves
   Note: For a more consistent look on the borders, use a fat quarter (22cm) per border.

6¼ yards (5.75m) backing fabric
⅝ yard (60cm) binding fabric
16—18" (45cm) squares of batting
2—10" x 82" (25cm x 2.08m) rectangles of batting
2—10" x 66" (25cm x 1.7m) rectangles of batting
Mylar heat-resistant template plastic
Compass block templates on pages 122-123
Appliqué templates on page 124

*Compass fabric requirements if you wish the fabrics to
   be consistent within each block:
   ¾ yard (75cm) fabric for Small Points
   ½ yard (55cm) fabric for Medium Points
   ¾ yard (75cm) fabric for Large Points
   ¼ yard (25cm) fabric for Centers

Cutting

From the Mylar plastic, cut:
   Center template on page 122
From background fabric, cut:
   64—Background Corners
   64—Background Corners Reversed
   256—Background Wedges
From compass fabric, cut:
   128—Small Points
   64—Medium Points
   64—Large Points
   16—4" squares for the block centers
From frame A fabric, cut:
   40—2½" x 17¼" rectangles
From frame B fabric, cut:
   40—2½" x 17¼" rectangles
From the border fabric, cut:
   8—6½" strips. Trim the selvages and
   join the strips into one continuous length.
   Press the seams open and cut:
      4—6½" x 64½" border strips
      4—8½" squares
      3—5¼" squares. Subcut the squares twice on the
         diagonal to make 12 quarter-square triangles.
      4—2⅞" squares. Subcut each square once on the
         diagonal to make 8 half-square triangles.
From the appliqué vine fabric, cut:
   1"-wide bias strips. Join the strips into one
   continuous length using diagonal seams. You will
   need approximately 480" (12.5m)
From the backing fabric, cut:
   16—18" squares
   8—10" strips. Trim the selvages and
   join the strips into one continuous length.
   Press the seams open and cut:
      2—10" x 82" strips
      2—10" x 66" strips
From the binding fabric, cut:
   9—2 1/2" strips.

Method

Making the Blocks

1. Lay out 4 background corners, 4 background corners reversed, 8 small points, 4 medium points and 4 large points as shown.

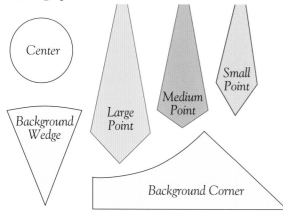

2. Layer a background corner and a background corner reversed, right sides together, and sew along the short edge. Press the seams open. Repeat with the remaining 3 pairs of background corners.

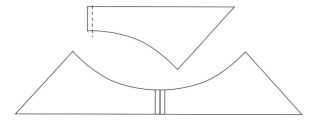

3. Layer 2 pairs of background corners, right sides together, and sew along one angled side to create a mitered corner. Press the seams open to create one half of the background square. Repeat with the remaining pair of background corners.

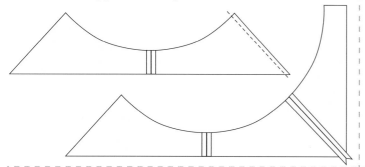

4. Layer the 2 background square halves, right sides together, and sew along each angled edge. Press the seams open to create the background square.

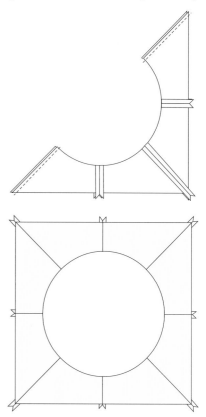

5. Layer a small point on top of a background wedge, right sides together, along one long raw edge as shown. Since the pieces are not the same length, there will be 1/4" of the background wedge visible at the top and bottom of the layered pieces. Sew the pieces together along the long raw edge. Press the seams toward the background wedge.

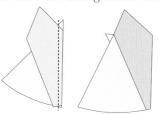

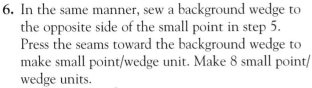

6. In the same manner, sew a background wedge to the opposite side of the small point in step 5. Press the seams toward the background wedge to make small point/wedge unit. Make 8 small point/wedge units.

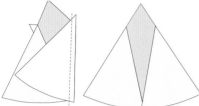

7. Layer a medium point on a small point/wedge unit, right sides together, along one long raw edge as shown. Sew the pieces together along the long raw edge. Press the seams toward the small point/wedge unit.

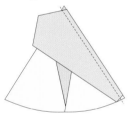
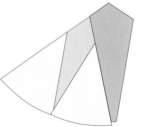

8. Layer a small point/wedge unit on the piece made in step 7, right sides together. Sew along one long raw edge as shown. Press the seams toward the small point/wedge unit to make a quarter wedge. Make 4 quarter wedges.

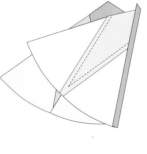

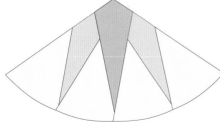

Note: At this point, it is helpful to lay out the block pieces again. This will insure that the large points are being sewn to the same side of each quarter wedge.

9. Layer a large point on a quarter wedge, right sides together, along one long raw edge. Begin sewing at the narrow edge of the large point and stopping ¼" from the raw edge as shown. Press the seams toward the quarter wedge to make a segment. Make 4 segments. Make sure the large point is sewn to the same side of each quarter wedge.

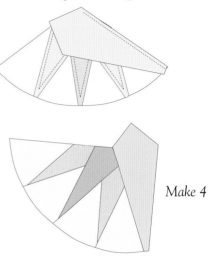

Make 4

10. Layer 2 segments, right sides together. Sew along one raw edge beginning at the narrow edge of the long point and stopping ¼" from the raw edge that will form the center of the block. Press the seams toward the background wedge.

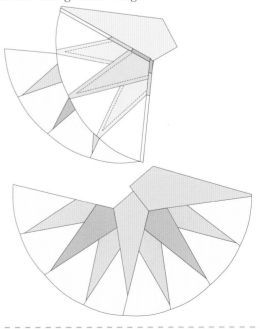

11. Continue sewing the remaining 2 segments to the piece made in step 10, stopping ¼" from the raw edge and pressing the seams toward the background wedges. When the 4 segments have been sewn together they will form a circle.

12. To complete the center circle, sew the wide edges of the large points together in pairs. Sew the pairs together straight across the center pressing the seam allowances in opposite directions.

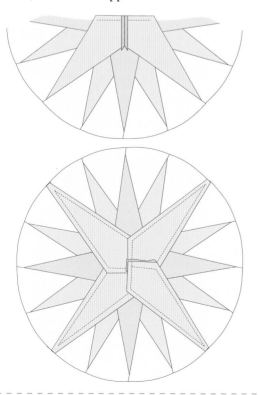

13. Position the center circle inside the background square, matching the points on the center circle with the seams on the background square. Pin along the matched points and seams first and then pin the points in between.

Stitch the pieces together with the center circle laying flat on the bed of the machine so you can see how the curved background fabric is easing in.

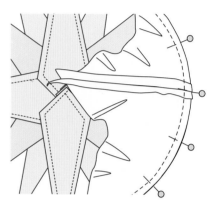

14. Press the seams away from the center circle.

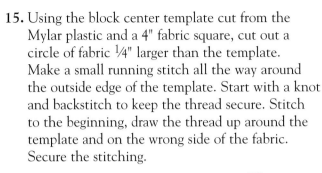

15. Using the block center template cut from the Mylar plastic and a 4" fabric square, cut out a circle of fabric ¼" larger than the template. Make a small running stitch all the way around the outside edge of the template. Start with a knot and backstitch to keep the thread secure. Stitch to the beginning, draw the thread up around the template and on the wrong side of the fabric. Secure the stitching.

16. Press with a warm iron to complete the circle shape. Remove the template.

17. Pin the circle in the center of the block and stitch down with a matching thread and small stitches. Press to complete the Mariners Compass block. Make 16 Mariners Compass blocks.

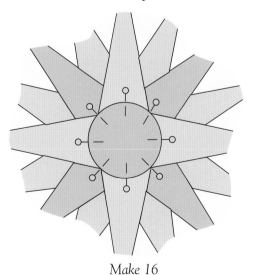

Make 16

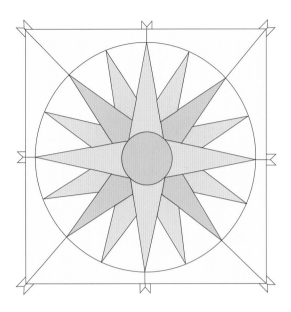

Adding the Frames

1. Using the 45-degree angle on a rotary cutting ruler, trim the corners of the 2½" x 17¼" frame A and B rectangles as shown. Set aside 8 trimmed A rectangles and 8 trimmed B rectangles for the borders.

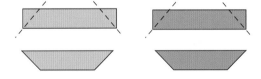

2. Sew the frames to the block referring to Mitered Corner Frames on page 36. Make 16 framed blocks.

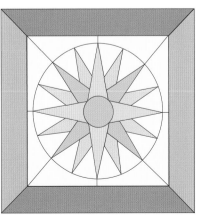

Make 16

Quilting the Framed Blocks

Referring to the diagram, quilt in the ditch around the block center circle and outline quilt the compass points. Use radiating lines to fill in the background. Quilt ¼" from the seam in the frame.

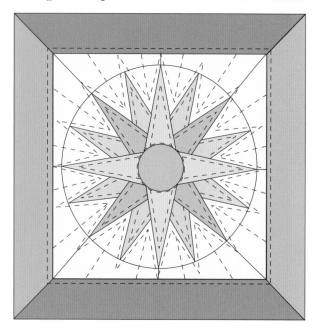

Completing the Quilt Center

1. Lay out the framed blocks in 4 rows with 4 blocks in each row. Sew the blocks together in rows referring to page 47.

2. Sew the rows together referring to page 51 to make the quilt center. Fill in the remaining quilting 1" from the seam of the frames and ¼" from where the blocks are joined together. Do not add more quilting around the outside edges of the quilt center as you still have to add the border.

Making the Borders

1. Lay out 2 half-square triangles, 2 trimmed frame A rectangles, 3 quarter-square triangles and 2 trimmed frame B rectangles as shown. Sew the pieces together and press the seams toward the frame rectangles to make an inner border. Make 4 inner borders.

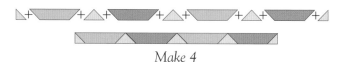

Make 4

2. Sew an inner border and 6½" x 64½" border strip together. Press the seams toward the border strip to make a pieced border strip. Make 4 pieced border strips.

Make 4

3. Sew an 8½" square to opposite ends of a pieced border strip. Press the seams toward the squares to make a side border. Make 2 side borders.

Make 2

4. Fold the continuous bias strip into thirds, wrong sides together, and baste together with long stitches to make a vine. The basting stitches will be removed later.

5. Using the photo on page 125 as a guide, lay the vine along a border. Pin the vine in place on the border, cutting off the excess vine. Repeat for each border, running the vine off the ends of the side borders if desired. From the remaining vine, create stems by cutting the vine into pieces and tucking them under the vine. Hand or machine applique the vines and stems in place. Remove the basting stitches.

6. Using the templates on page 124, cut out any number of flowers and leaves you wish to add to the borders. I used the same 4 flowers on each border and then filled the vine with leaves, but you may wish to mix up or add more flowers and use fewer leaves.

7. Using your favorite appliqué method, appliqué the flowers and leaves in place along the border vines. I used the freezer paper method since I prefer to hand appliqué.

Quilting the Borders

1. Layer the borders, batting and backing strips together. Quilt the borders remembering to stop quilting approximately 2" from any edge that will be sewn to another. For example, the ends of the two short borders and along the side where the frames join the border.

2. I outline quilted around the applique shapes and then marked 45-degree lines 10 apart starting in the center of each side of the border. I marked the corners on the long borders by outline quilting the seams of the square and filling the square with 1" cross hatching. This way the quilting lines from each border did not need to match up at the corners.

Finishing the Quilt

1. Sew the pieced border strips to the top and bottom of the quilt center using the Joining and Quilting the Rows method on page 51. Complete the quilting between the borders and the quilt center.

2. In the same manner, sew the side borders to the sides of the quilt center. Complete the quilting.

3. Sew the binding strips together on the diagonal to make one long continuous strip. Press the strip, wrong sides together, along the length. Sew the binding to the quilt referring to page 52. Add a label.

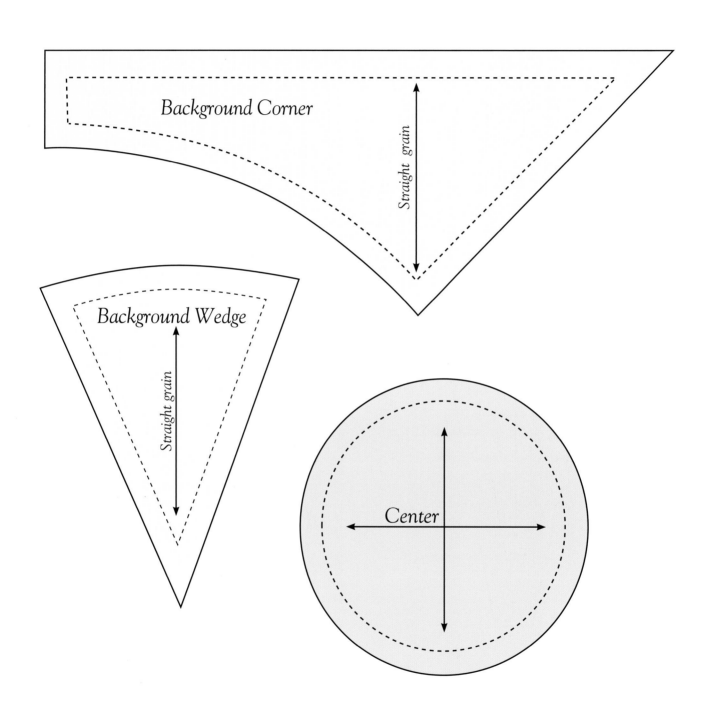

Background Corner

Straight grain

Background Wedge

Straight grain

Center

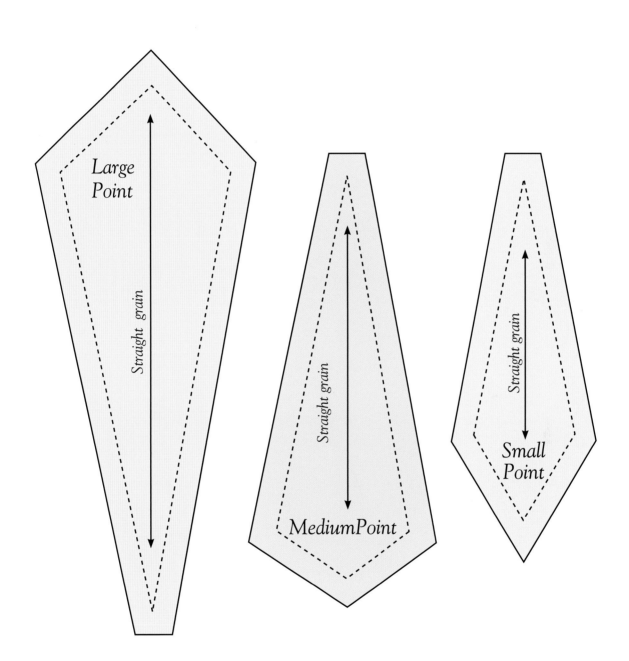

Large
Point

Straight grain

Straight grain

MediumPoint

Straight grain

Small
Point

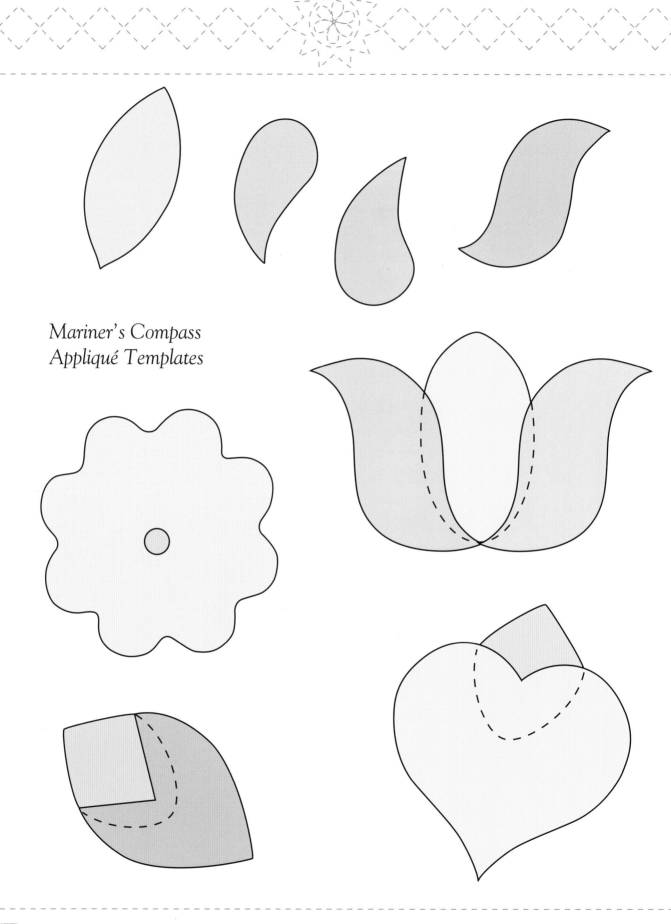

Mariner's Compass
Appliqué Templates

Mariner's Compass Quilt

Quilt Size: 80" x 80"

Resources

Batting
www.hobbsbatting.com

Quilting Thread
www.superiorthreads.com
www.valdani.com

505 Spray Baste
http://www.odifusa.com

Heat Press Batting Together Tape
www.heatpressbattingtogether.com

Hera Marker
www.clover-usa.com

Needles
www.jjneedles.com

American Folk Art Museum
www.folkartmuseum.org

Rotary Cutting Templates
for Mariner's Compass, Mayflower,
and Rolling Star blocks
www.Sew-Craft.com

Books

Quilting-on-the-Go,
Carolyn Forster, Landauer Publishing, 2007

Utility Quilting,
Carolyn Forster, Landauer Publishing, 2011

501 Rotary-Cut Quilt Blocks,
Judy Hopkins, That Patchwork Place, 2008

The Quilter Album of Patchwork Patterns,
Jinny Beyer, Breckling Press, 2009

Quiltmaking by Hand,
Jinny Beyer, Breckling Press, 2003

Quilting with Style,
Gwen Marston and Joe Cunningham,
AQS, 1993

Civil War Quilts,
Pam Weeks and Don Beld,
Schiffer Publishing, 2012

**Legacy: The story of
Talula Gilbert Bottoms and Her Quilts,**
Nancilu B. Burdick,
Rutledge Hill Press Publishing, 1998

Acknowledgements

Thank so much to Jeramy Landauer and her team at Landauer Publishing. When they agreed to take on my first Quilting-on-the-Go book, who knew where it would lead or how much fun it would be working with the Landauer team?

Thanks also to the students from my Quilting-on-the-Go classes who kept asking when the next book would come out, to which I replied, 'don't hold your breath'.

Thank you to everyone who has told me what a difference the quilting-on-the-go method has made in their quilting lives. It lets me quilt anywhere and make more quilts, and I'm so happy it does for you, too.

About the Author

Carolyn Forster, quilt maker, teacher and author, has been sewing and creating for as long as she can remember. Since stitching her first quilt from 1" fabric squares at the age of 17, she has been hooked on patchwork and quilting.

Carolyn's love of quilting sends her to many places teaching, lecturing and sharing her favorite quilting techniques. She has authored a number of patchwork and quilting books in the UK and America. Carolyn lives in Royal Tunbridge Wells, in the south east of England, with her husband and son, and a lot of fabric.